YESHUA

A DIFFERENT STORY

BY JOHN HULBERT

Yeshua: A Different Story

Copyright ©2019 by John Hulbert

All rights reserved.

Printed in the U.S.A.

Book design and cover: Michelle Radomski: www.onevoicecan.com

No part of this book may be reproduced or transmitted in any form or by any means, electronic or mechanical, including photocopying, recording or by any information storage and retrieval system without written permission of the publisher, except for the inclusion of brief quotations in a review.

Warning – Disclaimer

The purpose of this book is to educate and entertain. The author and/or publisher does not guarantee that anyone following the techniques, suggestions, tips, ideas or strategies will become successful. The author and/or publisher shall have neither liability nor responsibility to anyone with respect to any loss or damage caused, or alleged to be caused, directly by the information in this book.

Endorsement – Disclaimer

Reference herein to any specific commercial products, process, or service by trade name, trademark, manufacturer, or otherwise, in no manner endorses or sponsors the products, processes or offerings.

ISBN (paperback): 979–8-9864473-0-8
ISBN (ebook): 979-8-9864473-1-5
Library of Congress Control Number: Pending

"What is this precious love and laughter
Budding in our hearts.
It is the glorious sound
Of a soul waking up!"

~ (Hafiz 1320–1389)

ACKNOWLEDGMENTS

The teachings of Chung Fu (Old Chinese) and Yeshua are the foundations for this book. They have inspired me and have enriched my spiritual life. *A Course in Miracles* (ACIM) is a modern spiritual text that resonates with these two masters and has lighted a path to Awakening.

There are many other teachers and organizations that have helped me along the journey. While they may seem separate from each other, they are all part of the One great teaching. Thank you so much.

To list just a few. In alphabetical order:

A Course in Miracles	Judaism
Meher Baba	Jean Klein
Sally Baldwin	Robert Kiyosaki
The Bible	Hal Lafler
Glynn Braddy	Lao Tzu
Buddhism	Landmark
Edgar Cayce	Marshall Lever
Andrew Cohen	Coach Lloyd
Victor Frankl	Ramana Maharshi
The Gnostic Bible	Mana New Zealand
Joel Goldsmith	New Zealand Men's Group
Lisa Greenwood	Norm Paulson
Stanislav Grof	Rumi
The Group-Mariposa	Helen Schucman
Hafiz	Socrates
Sandy Harrick	The Tao
David Hawkins	William Thetford
Abraham-Hicks	Eckart Tolle
Hinduism	Neale Donald Walsch

Donald Walters   Paramahansa Yogananda
Kenneth Wapnick   Gary Zukav
Alan Watts

I had wonderful help in putting this book together. Eva Adams gave general advise and helped with the cover. Emma Routley helped in editing. Aleta Carpenter, once again, edited every page and paragraph making the book much clearer and grammatically correct.

Michelle Radomski and her husband Joe formatted the manuscript, created the cover, and did all things necessary to get it to publishing. Michelle can be reached at michelle@onevoicecan.com Holly Ostrout was most helpful in positioning the book and marketing. Reach Holly at holly@fictionalchemy.com Heartfelt thanks to you all.

TABLE OF CONTENTS

PART I — The Story of Yeshua

Introduction 1
Chapter 1   The Origin 3
Chapter 2:   Background 11
Chapter 3:   Yeshua: His Beginnings and First 30 Years 25
Chapter 4:   The Nazarene 33
Chapter 5:   Questions and Answers 51
Post Script   67

PART II — Yeshua Today

Introduction 75
Chapter 6:   Our Origin 77
Chapter 7:   The Universe 83
Chapter 8:   Time and Space 87
Chapter 9:   Reality 91
Chapter 10: Love 95
Chapter 11: Guilt 101
Chapter 12: Fear 105
Chapter 13: Forgiveness 109
Chapter 14: Judgment 113
Chapter 15: Gratitude 117
Chapter 16: Cause and Effect 119
Chapter 17: Ego 123
Chapter 18: Religion 129
Chapter 19: Resurrection 139
Chapter 20: Sickness 141
Chapter 21: Suffering 145
Chapter 22: Activism 149
Chapter 23: Awareness 155

Chapter 24: Death and Reincarnation 159
Chapter 25: The Way Forward 165
About the Author 169

— PART 1 —
THE STORY OF YESHUA

— PART 1 —
INTRODUCTION

The story of Yeshua (Jesus' actual Aramaic/Hebrew name) is not the commonly known Biblical story of his life, but is possibly the true and accurate story. It is significantly different and may come as a shock…be prepared. However, Yeshua's real message is one of great inspiration and hope.

This story is based on notes and transcripts of a channeling that took place in the mid-1970's by medium Marshall Lever. Lever's spirit guide, Chung Fu, was a student of Chuang Tzu (creator of the Tao teaching) in ancient China. The name Chung Fu was chosen from the *I Ching* and means "Inner Truth." Chung Fu emphatically pointed out that his teachings and guidance were not the only way but one of the many ways that individuals may take in their journey toward Inner Truth. He taught that there must be an unfolding within ourselves and an awareness of Inner Truth through meditation and self-discipline.

During the 70s, a full trance channeling took place over a weekend in California. Some of the references and attitudes were prevalent during the 70's at the time of this material being presented. Chung Fu consulted the Akashic records to provide an accurate account of Yeshua's life and teachings. Attendees gave a pledge not to reveal the story of Yeshua and his teachings until 33 years had passed, which is why the story is just now available.

While the material from Chung Fu's trance readings have been highly edited by me, the actual words in Part I of this book are all Chung Fu's. The Postscript at the end of Part I are my words.

The Story of Yeshua begins with a background of the hundreds of years proceeding Yeshua's appearance on the earth. The context of Judea and its history is necessary to understand what Yeshua encountered when he incarnated into the earth plane over 2,000 years ago.

His life story and message is remarkable and according to Chung Fu his teachings were without an ego. He was possibly the purest soul to live in our memory.

— CHAPTER 1 —
THE ORIGIN

Our story begins around 1800 B.C., with many tribes wandering the deserts of Egypt. Abraham was the patriarch of these wandering people. The people listened to what Abraham had to say as he talked of a God: Yahweh. He was the spokesman for God; the one Yahweh spoke through, tested, and reviewed. It was Abraham who gave inspiration to the many nomadic tribal individuals who were to become Jews. This was the beginning of the Jewish nation, although at this time they were simply nomadic tribes moving throughout the deserts of Egypt and North Africa. But each tribe had Yahweh, an almighty God presented and only contacted through Abraham. Yahweh was the key force, their strong energy, and their base.

Egypt, in its quest for slaves, began to raid the nomadic tribes throughout these areas. They brought the slaves to Egypt to build the temples and the great pyramids.

The captured tribes were pulled together and placed in prison camps in outlying communities near the great metropolises of Memphis and Thebes. They were not a Jewish nation yet, just nomadic tribes suddenly thrown together as slaves working and building gigantic monuments of stone. It was these nomadic tribes, forced into slavery, who lost Abraham. They had no leader, only one another. They suffered hardship and pain and developed hatred toward the soldiers, the architects, and the Pharaoh himself.

Some 500 years after Abraham, from Pharaoh's house, came Moses. Moses was one of the slaves, found as a baby on a stream that flowed by Pharaoh's palace and into the Nile. He had been placed there by his mother to avoid the Pharaoh's edict to kill all newborn Jewish babies in his effort to control the growing and dangerous Jewish population. Adopted by the daughter of Pharaoh and eventually by Pharaoh himself, Moses grew in stature and power. Although the Pharaoh's son was next in line, Moses became the new leader and came to rule over all of Egypt.

There was much turmoil in Egypt at this time. Many other nations were being built and Egypt was trying to maintain its own power base. It was in 1250 B.C. that Moses, who had felt empathy for the Jewish slaves, began to feel a part of their group and eventually led them out of Egypt. Taking on the energy of Abraham, Moses became the interpreter and the speaker of God, of Yahweh.

They wandered from settlement to settlement, with Moses teaching of the one God, Yahweh, and trying to harden them. The exodus was not as it is written. It was one of initiation for those who could make the journey. They spent forty years, but they spent it in getting rid of the dead wood, of allowing people who stayed to feel their strength and unity. For years Moses led them. He led them to the promised land, to Judea. But because of who he was, as a spiritual master, he turned away and went into solitude and they went into the promised land without him.

Still, they were not yet a Jewish nation. They were a collection of individuals who had been in prison for years. They had been disciplined and pulled into the single worship of Yahweh, the all-powerful God, who was in all things and who had a spokesman at all times. They went into Judea. There rose a prophet called Samuel, and God again spoke through him and Samuel appointed Saul as the king of all of these individuals.

In 1000 BCE, Saul was the king but it was Samuel who ruled. He was the prophet and prophets were the interpreters of God. If God spoke, He spoke through the prophets. There was no temple, no synagogue. It was only through the prophets, whether it was Ezekiel, or Amos, or Samuel. Samuel deposed Saul and brought forward David, and made David King of Judea. When David had Bathsheba's husband, Uriah, killed, Samuel had him flogged. Samuel gave David penance and told him who his heir would be. The heir could not be his son through Bathsheba; it must be Solomon. The prophet Samuel ruled. He was the interpreter and he was the projector of God. It was under Solomon that Nathan the prophet took over from Samuel and the temple was built.

Jerusalem was not a metropolis. It was a town of scattered houses, a place where people met, and a marketplace. It was not something to behold and say "Isn't it beautiful?" But Solomon built a temple there anyway. There was not beauty in Jerusalem, just low rock hills where a temple to Yahweh was built.

Solomon became the king, the ruler and the spokesman for Yahweh, replacing the prophet and taking on many wives, renewing his energy through the feminine source. He brought thousands of women to him to become his wives - his concubines. He did not listen to Nathan or to any of the prophets. He was the representative of Yahweh. He built the temple. He began to develop the priesthood of Sadducee. With Solomon's death impending, there was a division within his house between Rehoboam, Solomon's son, and Jeroboam, an official of Solomon. Jeroboam had earlier fled to Egypt after trying to usurp power from Solomon.

Upon the death of King Solomon (931 BCE), Solomon's son, Rehoboam, took over the kingdom. The ten Northern tribes rebelled against the government of Rehoboam and asked Jeroboam to rule as king. Jeroboam became king of the ten Northern tribes and refuted the temple of Solomon in Jerusalem. He established his own golden calf idols to which the ten northern tribes paid homage and gave offerings. Rehoboam believed in the prophets and thought he was the sole heir to Solomon. He believed what

Zachariah, Amos, and Nehemiah said, that King Solomon brought the wrath of Yahweh upon Israel by turning to idolatry and that he, Rehoboam, was the true heir. The nation was still not Jewish, but did center its worship of Yahweh in Solomon's temple in Jerusalem; worshiping only one God. The kingdom was divided between Northern (Kingdom of Israel) and Southern (Kingdom of Judah). For many years the kingdom was torn in two with Jeroboam, Rehoboam, and their descendents fighting back and forth.

Over a period of years, Yahweh took a backseat to many small trinket gods. There were altars for this god and that: the corn god, the street god, the house god, the tree god, the animal god. Incense was burned for each of them. The temple was still there and Yahweh dwelled within it. His energy was there, protected by the Sadducee priesthood, which was hereditary.

In 722 BCE the Assyrian Empire conquered Judea, and for the first time in almost a thousand years, Judea found itself under foreign rule. The people were suppressed and had nothing to unify them, for they had forsaken Yahweh for the little gods. They would still sacrifice in the temple, while the Assyrians gave them even more gods. No king ruled but Nehemiah and the prophets of Israel who were still speaking for Yahweh, still speaking to the people and trying to get them to take notice, said that the Assyrians were good for them. The prophets believed it was a punishment of Yahweh.

Then in 587 BCE the Babylonian Empire began, the strongest empire to date. Nebuchadnezzar, the king, went to Jerusalem and took every main leader, every main priest from the temple, and every individual who had any leadership ability back to Babylon. He did not imprison them but gave them jobs, allowing them to make money and to become a part of the Babylonian Empire. This was his pattern with every nation he conquered: He would take the leaders back to his main city and offer them money-making opportunities and positions of loyalty.

Babylon was the center and the source point at that time. It was the Paris, the London, the New York, the Rome, the Athens, and the San Francisco, all in one. And Jerusalem was a little town in the Midwest someplace. They were now in exile, but they weren't in exile in discomfort. If completely assimilated this could have brought the end to everything Judaic, but it was in exile from 587–537 BCE that Judaism was born, not before.

During this same time brought the world Confucius, Lao Tzu, and Buddha, and just a few years later Socrates, Plato, and Teotihuacan. Within Babylon it was Zoroaster and within Rome it was Pythagoras.

Dutra Isaiah, the greatest and most powerful prophet of all Judaic faiths, was now in Babylon. First created were the family units called the synagogues. They established that within the home you could worship God or Yahweh since he was in all things everywhere. You did not need to go to the temple in Jerusalem; you could worship at home

Dutra Isaiah wrote prolifically, describing the future and what had to be done, that Yahweh was the light and the all powerful God. Here in Babylon the word Yahweh began to be such a powerful energy that it could not be muttered or said out loud by anyone. You did not mention the name Yahweh, but Yahweh was in the home, for the altar was in the home, and to be a teacher you became a rabbi in a synagogue.

Listening to all the stories, the Jewish leaders began to pull together their history and to write the Old Testament. They began to compile the stories and put together everything that the Old Testament is today. It was written at this time. The Pentateuch was put together. Dutra Isaiah wrote the basis of all the Old Testament in the second part of Isaiah. From the Assyrians, the Hittites, and the Mesopotamians he took the story of the beginnings. He took the double genesis story from the Hittites.

The ten commandments were a combination of what the Hittites, the Mesopotamians, and the Assyrians offered. It was not given to Moses on top of a mountain but was a conglomeration of laws that filtered through the great trade routes from Babylon to India. The Jewish leaders began to write the genesis story, the beginnings, based on what they learned from other nations, other tribes, different religions, even from what they had heard from Buddha and his Sangra in India.

Zoroaster was prominent in Babylon. He taught and preached that the cosmic force was always at battle between the dark and light forces. He taught everlasting life and he taught sin: the bad and the good. He taught eternal damnation for not seeking the beauty of Self. These beliefs became the traditions of the Judaic faith, part of its oral tradition. The people believed and they accepted it.

In the little synagogues, the little homes that were throughout Babylon, Seder would be celebrated; the journey of Moses. They would break bread, pour wine, and say, "Break bread and may all that are here partake. Here, the bread is the body of man and wine is the blood of man."

In Babylon the Torah was formed and the laws were created. Judaism came into being. In Babylon three great world religions were formed; Judaism, Christianity eventually, and Islam. They evolved from Judaism; from those individuals who had been brought to exile by Nebuchadnezzar.

Then in 538 BCE Cyrus invaded Babylon, releasing the Jews and letting them return to Jerusalem. Many did not want to go because they were making large amounts of money. They were comfortable within the metropolis of Babylon. Dutra Isaiah, their prophet and organizer, had just died. But they had a Bible; a compilation of books they had put together. They had their history; a conglomeration of poems and verses, and stories as told by the Mesopotamians, the Hittites, the Assyrians, the Hindus and those of the trade routes who came to Babylon.

The ten commandments were in direct alignment with the laws of the ancient Assyrians. The Jews created a priesthood called Pharisees within Babylon, which was a direct derivative of those who followed Zoroaster, called Pharsees. The Pharsees were different from the Pharisees, who eventually became the priesthood in Jerusalem.

These were the origins of Judaism and the exile was over. The handful of people who left Babylon for the 600-mile journey to Jerusalem were filled with the excitement that they were taking the true faith with them. They were bringing to Jerusalem, to the people who they had left so long ago, the true Yahweh, His power and strength, and everything they had attained. They were excited like little children upon their journey, but upon reaching Jerusalem these returning Jews found they were not accepted; they were considered radicals and idiots. So, the returnees began their hard and difficult work.

During this period of time a great energy influx arrived to allow the earth plane to continue working. In India Buddha developed a priesthood of celibate beings called the Sangra. The Sangra allowed people to have a meditative source and create a vibrational force through the eight fold path. In China Lao Tzu developed the Tao I Ching which said that which is, isn't, and that which isn't, is; meaning that your body isn't and that what isn't your body is. For example, your body is an illusion and your soul is your reality. Also, in China Confucius allowed strength to come to the empire, giving a legal perspective. The Judaic faith pulled together the one God of all, one invisible Yahweh. Pythagoras learned all of these.

From Persia Zoroaster projected strength and insisted that there was life after death. There was return. There was sin, there was evil and there was good. You had to repent and constantly work against the overpowering of evil. This was the beginning of the Suphic schools of Socrates and Plato, and of Teotihuacan in the Americas.

All of these individuals, including Dutra Isaiah, were perceived as fools, as individuals who were bad for the society in which they were working because they rocked the boat. They caused imbalances, irregularities, and difficulties—great difficulties. This was the major overhaul for this cataclysmic period.

The 500 years from 537 B.C. to the time of Yeshua were the most crucial for the Judaic religion. What happened in Jerusalem and its surroundings during this period help make Yeshua what he was.

— CHAPTER TWO —
BACKGROUND

When Cyrus conquered Babylon at the beginning of the Persian Empire, he released the Jews, or those who had become Jews and were in Babylon, and told them that they could return to Jerusalem. Only the most fervent, the strongest, and the most missionary people of the group, who had meticulously assembled the Old Testament, re-aligned the Pentateuch, and were now developing the theory and basis of the Pharisee Party, left Babylon. This is similar to the world today, in that only those who have the fortitude and the energy to live with great challenge and balance go back to Israel.

Most of the Jews today live in major cities throughout the world and so it was in Babylon. Upon returning they found they were not accepted. There was a group of individuals already residing in Jerusalem called Samaritans, who were pushing the Torah as the central element of their religious fervor.

The Samaritans were a strong group. They were Jewish, or we will call them Jewish following the developments brought about by Dutra Isaiah in Babylon. But the Pharisee Party—the Pharisees—was a priesthood that possessed a group of strong leaders who eventually came into power with the support of

Cyrus and the Persians. These leaders (Ezra, Jeremiah, Haggai), began a centralization of the faith, establishing an understanding and a core energy.

The Pharisees introduced the synagogue, the family structure, which was completely new to the Samaritans. The Samaritans were actually the stronger group and considered this usurping group from Babylon to be betraying the whole tradition of the Promised Land. The Pharisees began to solidify their rules and regulations and were strongly advocating for their beliefs. Coming from Babylon, they felt—as did Judea—that they were the chosen people and that one day they would rule the world. Dutra Isaiah inspired Isaiah to say that these people will rule the world and all the world will serve them. And so from the depth of their belief, this core group of all Judaism began to believe this.

As this great thought began to take root, they also conceived the idea that there was going to be a Messiah. The direct translation is "Anointed One": one who would lead them to a state of being completely in charge of their existence and thereby being the THE POWER within the world. Every Pharisee believed and taught this, even though it was not mentioned within the OLD Testament or the Pentateuch.

Everyone believed that the Messiah, the Chosen One, was going to come tomorrow. The Samaritans believed it also, but in a different form. The Pharisees believed in angels. They had a hierarchy of angels and spiritual elements of the earth, the air, and the water. Pharisees believed in communicating with the dead and developed a verbal belief that you could communicate to those who were passing. If you died and had been a strict and aligned Jew, you stayed in a state of suspended animation. As long as your ancestors and your family continually used your name in the temple you were on "hold," so to speak, until the Messiah came and led a great world revolution. They believed strongly and completely that they would return and that they would rule the world as the great leaders had, but that they would do it for eternity. The arrival of the Messiah was expected the next morning or the next second. During this time Jerusalem slowly became a pulsating center, the crossroads of the known world.

Many of the present-day songs of Christianity talk about a land far away. This is not true, for Jerusalem sat in the middle of the great empires of the Mediterranean and was the center trading post to the East and to the West. If you travelled between trading posts—if you traveled at all—you came to Jerusalem. If you were going from North to South, you went through Jerusalem. It had no agricultural significance. It was a religious center only. In the center was a rock, the rock where Abraham was supposed to have sacrificed his son Isaac and where at the last moment Abraham received a reprieve from God. This was back in 1800 B.C. when the Jews were only a nomadic tribe.

The Persians ruled Judea and Jerusalem and supported the Pharisees. On returning to Judea in 537 BCE, the Pharisees instituted changes, allowing the Judaic tradition to be more individualized. The Samaritans feared that the Pharisees were bringing in new ideas, and when the Pharisees passed a law that every Jew had to divorce any woman who was not Jewish, the Samaritans revolted and moved away. The Samaritans no longer kept any association with Jerusalem and Judea, although they still believed in the Torah. As the men divorced those wives who were not of the lineage, who were not of one of the many tribes that had eventually come together and created this nation, a national solidity began.

The temple that Solomon built had been ruined, so the Pharisees had to worship in little enclaves here and there. The "meal" was developed and the Pharisee tradition of the Sabbath, Saturday, the seventh day of rest. And so on Friday night the family would gather together and break bread and dedicate it to the body. Then at the end of the meal they would drink wine. This meal became the key, the core of Judaism. Each time that they would gather together for the meal they would wait for the joyous day when the Messiah would lead them out of the persecution of the

Persians and into the world dominance that they had believed for so many centuries.

The world conqueror, Alexander the Great, came to Jerusalem and talked to the people. He brought to the Pharisees the wisdom of the Greek philosophers Socrates, Plato, and others, and appropriated some of their feelings and thoughts into the Pharisees beliefs. The Pharisees incorporated the Hellenistic ideal within their traditions. Alexander allowed everything to remain intact. He ruled strongly and developed Alexandria, which became a city and replaced Babylon as the metropolitan center of the world.

It was in Alexandria that the Old Testament was translated into Greek. And it was here that much of the meaning of the Hebrew tradition, in translation, was misinterpreted and misunderstood. It was called the Septuagint. It was here, out of Isaiah, that came one of the most flagrant misrepresentations which in the future throughout the world has caused many problems. In Hebrew the word means "young woman," but translated into the Greek it became "virgin." In Hebrew it stated "and he will come forth from a young woman," NOT "and he will come forth from a virgin."

During this time there were more Jews in Alexandria than there were in Jerusalem, just as today there are more Jews in New York than there are in Jerusalem. Alexandria became the intellectual center of the empire. Following Alexander's reign, a Hellenistic King entered Jerusalem in approximately 175 BCE. His name was Antiochus. He defiled the temple, slaughtering pigs throughout and forced the Jews and the Pharisees to do the same.

By 163 BCE the Jews rose up in a great revolt overthrowing the Hellenistic rule. For 100 years, from 163 to 63 BCE, Judea was an independent state run by a group called the Maccabees. It was a time of 100 years of peace; 100 years of Judaism. It was during this time that the temple became a center, although attempts had been made to re-build, it was still torn and ravaged. But the synagogues, or the home, became strong. During this period a man came forward called the Prophet of Righteousness, for no one knew his name. He was Essene in tradition and came from the Essene community. He was a powerful individual who solidified the Essenes and was as strong as Dutra Isaiah had been in Babylon. The Prophet of Righteousness worked within the Pharisee tradition, for he came from the Pharisees as all leaders did. He preached, not about a king, but about a ruler who would rule through the religious faith as Nathan, Samuel, Elijah, Eziah, and Nehemiah had.

A celibate and very strict community of Essenes developed in Qumran. They believed that only individuals who were drawn to it should be allowed to stay. They were not missionaries, but were a strong group pulled from the surrounding populace toward the great amount of energy and strength of this one individual who wrote about the Messiah. They believed that two Messiahs would come: a priest and a military leader.

Those who came to Qumran, if accepted into the group, had to lead a celibate life. Contrary to the sacrifices in the great temple in Jerusalem, they revised the Seder meal, or the Friday evening meal. Instead of sacrificing a lamb as was done in the temple, they would say, "Here is the bread, it is the body. Here is the wine, it is the blood. Therefore we do not have to sacrifice." They pulled the Essene group together and taught about life after death and communicated with the dead. They had individuals who could heal; individuals who were strong and powerful in their understanding of healing sources. People from all over Judea came to Qumran to be healed, for when they saw the power and the strength of the Essene they were pulled to it.

Yet the Essenes were not missionaries. They were silent about their actions, but because of the energy they created they became known. They, the Prophet of Righteousness, and the Pharisee Party wanted the Maccabees out of power, for the Maccabees had turned into kings. They had developed a monarchy, an authority over Yahweh, and no longer even spoke his name. It was a blasphemy and immediate death if one mentioned the name of Yahweh. Because he was all powerful in all things, any Jew who mentioned his name was immediately put to death. The Anointed One, God, the Beautiful One, and other pseudonyms were used.

Then in 63 BCE Pompey annexed Judea. The Jews fought, but Pompey knew that on Saturday they would not fight. So, on a Saturday, he stormed the gates of Jerusalem, went to the temple, and his guards began to slaughter the priests. For every one they killed another would step forward because it was the Sabbath and they had to protect the altar. To keep the altar sacred, 7,000 priests stepped forward that day, and 7,000 were slaughtered in front of the altar. Confused, Pompey could not understand why they did not fight; they just continued reading from their scriptures.

Once Pompey conquered the temple he looked around and saw a large curtain. It was behind this gigantic curtain that their god, Jehovah or Yahweh, was supposed to be. He stepped into the Holy of Holies, which only the High Priest was allowed to enter twice each year, on the Day of Atonement and on the Day of Passover. Pompey stepped into that room and saw nothing but a lot of dust. He looked around; it was dark and he was confused that there was nothing there.

At this point in time the Romans were the rulers of the world. They gave power and control for Judea to Herod the Great, and the seat of the political structure went to the coast, calling it Caesarea. No longer was any of the political energy centered in Jerusalem; it was simply the place of religion for the Jews. Caesarea became the place where Herod, the Roman governor, stayed. He only went to Jerusalem twice a year for Atonement and Passover to make sure that everything was under control. Caesarea, on the coast, was a powerful center. It was there that everything from the Roman world entered Judea and the fertile crescent. The energy of the Roman Empire was first felt in Caesarea which also contained the main troops and the head Tribune.

Herod the Great came to the throne in 37 BCE, and in the glory of the power that he felt, in a great egotistical flurry, he rebuilt the temple to a grandeur previously unseen. It was centered on the rock on top of Jerusalem in all its glory. When the temple was finished, all of the present day Vatican could fit inside of it. No matter where you stood in Jerusalem, the temple threw a shadow over the houses and streets.

The temple was the center and the power of the entire Jewish religion. The roofs of the inner court were solid gold sheets; when the sun shone upon them the glow was seen from far out at sea. There were towers in which lights were lit and the brilliance of the lights on the shining gold could be seen in the dark for miles.

The large court was called the Court of the Gentiles, and it was here that the people met. It had stalls where animals were bought and sold for sacrifice. It had money changers, for the temple had its own currency. You could not buy an animal for sacrifice or anything else within the temple without temple currency so you had to change your money there. It had its own priests, its own prison, and it was here in the Court of the Gentiles that any man who was of the Jewish faith and who was circumcised could teach or preach. It was the place of learning and it was the place where anyone of the Judaic faith could go to talk about what he believed. It was an open forum the size of three football fields.

You could walk among the teachers or the Pharisees to hear what they had to say; each one had a different point of view. You could listen to teachers who believed their way was the only way to interpret the Torah. Anyone who was of the Jewish faith could come to listen and walk and discover what was going on. As individuals would preach and talk in the Court of the Gentiles the ins and outs of their faith began. This was the center of all the Judaic faith. This was where the Pharisees taught and where the two major schools of Pharisaic thought were centered: the school of Hillel and the school of Shammai.

From the Court of the Gentiles you entered through a door into the Court of the Women, and up the stairway to the Court of Israel. Only circumcised men of the Jewish faith were allowed to ascend the stairs. The steps were red, and there were guards at every fourth one, who would challenge a man and ask to see his circumcision. Anyone not a circumcised Jewish male who attempted to walk up these stairs to the Holy of Holies would be killed on the spot.

The Court of Israel was a place for prayer, a place where you stood and waited before entering the Court of the Priests. In the center of the Court of the Priests was the stone altar upon which Abraham was supposed to have been ready to sacrifice Isaac. Here each and every Jew, every individual who had a strong Jewish faith, brought a sacrifice, at least three times each year, to be sacrificed upon this altar. It was like a butcher shop, but it was a sacrifice to Yahweh, whose room now stood behind the altar. The High Priest could only enter this Holy of Holies on the Day of Atonement or at Passover. He would enter with his robes of office and standing alone, he would utter the most sacred word "Yahweh." These were the only times in the whole year, and the high priest the only man who could mention the name Yahweh.

During the Passover, Jerusalem became a Mecca, a Rome, a Lourdes. It became a pilgrimage that each year every prominent Jew throughout the Roman Empire, the known world, would make the trip, at least twice, to sacrifice at the altar. During the Passover the head of every family had to sacrifice a lamb at the altar and the sacrifices started early. During the Passover more than 30,000 animals were sacrificed. This was a powerful time for the Judaic faith. The sacrifices were made daily; the temple trumpets of solid silver would blare over all of Jerusalem when the sacrifices commenced each morning. It was said that you could not talk while the trumpets were blaring, and they blared every fifteen minutes.

A prominent Jew would bring a sheep, a bird, or an ox to be slaughtered on the altar. The priest would take some of the fat and place it on the altar and give the animal back to the person who would then eat it immediately. During other sacrifices, birds or animals would be slaughtered but were not necessarily eaten. This was the core of the Judaic faith.

In this period, from 37 BCE to 4 BCE, the foundation was created for the appearance of Yeshua. The two main schools of the Pharisees, Hillel and Shammai, taught the Torah. Jews constantly worked with the Torah and read the laws. It became everyday knowledge much as the laws of driving are today. People knew the laws, what they could and could not do, such as how far they could walk on the Sabbath. The School of Hillel believed in the spirit of the Torah while the School of Shammai believed in a more strict interpretation of the Torah. They would argue back and forth fervently about what the Torah meant. These discussions were seen on every "street corner" in the Court of Gentiles. Men would come from all over the Roman world to study under Hillel or Shammai or some of the other teachers who would fence the Law with them to give them an understanding so that they could go back and teach in their own synagogues as a Rabbi.

The temple was rich, for every Jewish community sent money regularly which arrived daily. The treasure house of the temple was wealthier than the Roman Emperor, Julius Caesar.

Beit Hillel, the Pharisee teacher, believed in the coming of the Messiah and his teaching reflected this belief. Beit Shammai also believed in the coming of the Messiah but in a little more technical form. Another party, the Sadducee, were the leaders of the temple, and the head priest was from this party. These were the political leaders and the individuals who ran the temple. The head priest was the one permitted to enter the Holy of Holies to speak the word "Yahweh," but he could only do this wearing the temple robes of the High Priest. The Roman ruler kept the robes until the Day of Atonement or the Day of the Passover, so the Head Priest only had them two days a year. This meant that Rome controlled the High Priest. The Sadducees were a conservative group who dealt with the political elements of the Law, of the Torah. They were not Parasitic, for they did not believe in the interpretation of the

Law by word of mouth as the Pharisees did; they believed in the depth of the Law. Also, they did not believe in the Messiah as they were very conservative.

There was also a militant party called the Zealots. They believed that if you did not follow the Law, that if you worked for the Romans or Herod, you needed to be killed and slaughtered. They were the assassins among the Jews, and many prominent Jews who spoke to Herod's men or to the Romans, found themselves on the Zealots' black list. The Zealots believed the Messiah was going to be a great political leader, overthrow Rome, and rule the entire world.

During the period of 37 BCE, when Herod came to the throne, to 4 BCE, when he died, there were no less than 100 different Jewish parties and small groups melding and causing animosity. Jerusalem and Judea were known as the sore spot of the Roman Empire. Jerusalem was a place where your life was not very worthwhile if you were Roman. The Pharisees had created the word of the Law and controlled the Judaic system, even though the Sadducee, or the priesthood, had control and the run of the temple. The Pharisee tradition ruled, and they were the ones in charge of the synagogues.

There were 20,000 priests of the temple and each man served at least twice in his lifetime as a priest. Levites were the underlying priests. They were the choir, they cleaned up the altar, and they made sure that things were kept in order.

The Essenes were a powerful group at Qumran by the Dead Sea, an area with very little water. The Teacher of Righteousness was assassinated here, both because of his strength and because of his power to solidify and pull people away from the Maccabee tradition.

To the south there was another Essene community called the Therapeutics, founded by Pythagoras, with both men and women as members. They were an open group of Essenes who were Judaic in tradition but who viewed men and women as equals. They were family oriented and believed in the family unit as its own source of strength. The Essene Therapeutics combined healing of the body with healing of the soul. At this time the Essenes believed in communication with the spirits, life after death, a heaven and a hell. They broke bread and drank wine as a symbol of the slaughter that went on in the temple. They did not believe in sacrificing lambs in the temple and so they broke the bread as the symbol of the body, and drank the wine as symbolic of the blood. They did not take any sacrifice to the altar as all Jews, including the Zealots, the Samaritans, the Sadducees, and Pharisees, did.

It has been thought by some scholars that the Teacher of Righteousness was actually Yeshua or that Yeshua was a figment of someone's imagination. This is not so. The Essene community at Qumran was well known; from this community came John the Baptist. John left the community because he believed that the power that they had created must be preached–it must be heard. So he broke with the Essene community, who had kept their beliefs to themselves and went away to preach and baptize, to wash away the old and to come to a new life. He felt that what the Essenes had learned must be shared. He taught what the Essenes did differently and he taught it flagrantly in public, unlike the Essene community at Qumran which taught it only for those who came and were eventually initiated into their celibate order.

The Zealots were moving about Judea and killing those who collaborated with the Romans. They were fervent in regards to the Judaic faith. They were also from the Pharisaic tradition. The Pharisees were in charge of all synagogues throughout the known world: Rome, Caesarea, Alexandria, and all parts of Greece. The two schools of Hillel and Shammai taught the Torah and it was within this fervor, within this energy, that Yeshua was born.

This was one of the most powerful points of time in all history, a melting pot of so many different cultures and religious thoughts that have not been seen since. Jerusalem was a crossroad and pulled in many different teachers. Judea was even more bubbling and boiling that it is now. From the time that the Jews came from Babylon they felt that they were the chosen people and were going to rule the world. They felt that they were going to be in charge of every nation and that they would do it even if they had to fight to do it. (Two thousand years later millions of them were killed by a man who thought the same thing.)

They believed this so strongly that every military government thought they were a threat and they were closely watched. Their leaders were watched. Any time a leader came forth with a new thought or a new feeling he was watched. The community of Qumran was watched. The Zealots, even though they were somewhat of a guerrilla group, were watched. Hillel was watched as was Shammai.

The Sadducee Party were those individuals who did anything they could to keep the status quo from overturning them and so they would bend left and right, forward and backward, depending upon which way the wind blew. It is interesting that the Pharisaic tradition still lives, but in 70 CE, when the temple was torn to the ground and destroyed, the Sadducee Party died and has never returned. But the Pharisaic tradition of Hillel and Shammai continued.

The Essene community was Judaic; they believed in the Torah, but they interpreted it in different ways. If you were a Jew, as a young man, you learned to debate the Torah. You learned the essence of the faith. You read the Torah and you read the scriptures that were available. Every young man did. This was a time of high energy and of great change.

In Egypt an individual named Phel was beginning to teach and bring forth ideas that were new and exciting in regards to life itself. One of his teachings at this time stated, "All men are created equal." He taught that if you wanted to have the best good done to you, you had to do the best good to all who came around you.

There was another group of individuals who were healers. They were healers of herbs and healers of the word; of the thought and of the view of life. They could stand before a person and by looking at him, could tell what was wrong with him. By putting a hand upon his shoulder and looking in his eyes they were able to pull out the negativity or the "evil spirit," so to speak. They would give him an herb and make him feel strong and powerful. They had a view of the future and knew their own strength. They were called sorcerers or magicians and one specific group was referred to as the Nazarites. They were a strong group and known throughout Judea.

If one of these sorcerers came into a community, the community flocked to him to be healed or to receive word about what was to come, for it always meant the community would have something new. The sorcerers were, of course, Jews and they had learned the Judaic tradition. They had come up within the temple and they believed in the Torah. Almost all were from the Pharisaic tradition. They were from the school of Hillel but also knew the herbs for healing and knew how to rid a person of their worries. They knew themselves, and their apprenticeship was strong. They traveled from the Essene Therapeutic community to a school in Damascus which dealt with some of the ancient traditions of the Pharaoh's physicians in the use and mixing of herbal potions. They were a mobile group not staying in one place for very long. They were in demand and there were never enough of them to meet the needs of the populace because of the strict criteria that had to be met in order to be a sorcerer. They were deeply a part of the Pharisaic tradition and not feared but understood, respected, and looked up to.

It was at the end of 8 BCE or the beginning of 7 BCE when Joseph married Mary. Joseph was almost 75 and Mary was 15. Joseph had had a wife who had died and with whom he had a large family. Joseph and Mary were married in the temple and in the faith. Joseph was a strong man, and soon after their marriage Mary became pregnant. In 7 BCE Yeshua was born–7 BCE. A confused monk in 385 CE changed the calendar. Yeshua had two sisters and four brothers, one of whom was an initiate in the Nazarites at the time of Yeshua's birth. Herod, who'd had all the young children killed, died in 4 BCE.

From the Hebrew tradition comes a word "neumder" which can be translated two ways: "carpenter" or "sorcerer." Joseph was actually a sorcerer, the head of the group mentioned above. The group's name was "The Nazarites." There was no Nazareth until 9 CE. Before this date the city did not even exist. Yeshua was born to a young mother, Mary, and was the son of Joseph, a sorcerer, who was the head of the Nazarites. Yeshua had an older brother, James, who was already an initiate in the Nazarites. This was one of the most crucial periods in history, before the death of Herod, at the peak of the Roman Empire and at the time of Augustus Caesar.

— CHAPTER THREE —

YESHUA: HIS BEGINNINGS AND FIRST THIRTY YEARS

Two billion people have either followed Yeshua or lived in lands that are influenced by him. More than 75,000 books have been written about him. More wars have been fought over his interpretations than over any other individual. Lives have been martyred and nations have been destroyed to a greater extent than for any other individual in our world.

Being a sorcerer, Joseph traveled continuously. He understood the elements of astrology and knew the astrological alignments which the Essenes understood and which the Zoroastrians also believed in. In 7 BCE there was an alignment of the planets that for a period of seven days and nights caused a great light to appear in the sky, a star that was brighter than all others. It was in this seven day period that Yeshua was born. Joseph, the sorcerer, knew it was time. He knew the sign and he knew the unique vibration of this time, for his contacts were not just in Jerusalem and Caesarea; he had travelled to Damascus, Egypt, Alexandria and even as far north as Samaria. He knew the signs well.

At the time of Yeshua's birth there were other sorcerers, wise men and astrologers, who visited Joseph and Mary. He was not born in a manger; he was born under an olive tree (which now symbolizes Peace) in route from one town to another. And there, for a period of seven days, astrologers and Nazarites came and gave acknowledgement and great support to Joseph and Mary.

Yeshua was born the son of a sorcerer and his younger years, until he was 12 years old, were spent in the Pharisee tradition. Yeshua was taught within the temple, learned the Torah and could debate it with the best of teachers. He spent many hours in the temple and in the Courts of the gentiles fencing with Hillel and sometimes Shammai. He supported and believed in all the Judaic teachings.

Yeshua was first a Jew and learned everything the temple had to teach. He was initiated between his twelfth and thirteenth year, circumcised and taken to the temple and up the stairs of the Court of Women, into the Court of Israel and finally into the Court of Priests where a lamb was sacrificed for him. After that time, his father Joseph, travelled with him far into the deserts to the south and left him in the community of the Therapeutic Essenes or what was then called the Family Essenes. Joseph, upon leaving him, told him that it was here he would learn the measure of people. He would learn of male and female, learn the law, and learn utilization of the vibration of earth, air, and water, and learn it well.

For eight years Yeshua dwelt there learning the ancient rituals including the ritual of breaking bread in the remembrance of the lamb and drinking the wine in remembrance of the blood of the lamb, rather than actually sacrificing it. He learned of communication beyond the dead. He believed in the coming of the Messiah, of the great teacher, the liberator of all Judea. He was an intelligent being, extremely so. He was not an individual who was ordained from the beginning. He came from the tradition of the East, the reincarnation of Zoroaster, to give an influx of energy to the earth plane at a particular time during the alignment of the earth and other planets.

The community of the Therapeutic Essenes was on the border with Egypt. While with the Essenes, Yeshua was learning how to cultivate a field, grow a flower, and the use of insects and animals. He was learning the communication between man and woman. He learned the discipline of self from his many wanderings in the desert. He learned the practice of eating little and gaining much in inspiration.

On his twenty-first birthday James, his older brother, came and got him from the Therapeutic Essenes. James took him to Damascus, and there, for a period of five years, Yeshua trained in the house of a physician; a physician who had come through the schools not only of Egypt but of Greece. He learned the mixes of herbs and essences. He learned of the healing sounds of water. He learned of the elements (fire, water, air and earth). He learned of the nature of people. His teacher was of the Pharisaic tradition and he watched and listened to this teacher well.

After five years in Damascus, James came to collect Yeshua. Joseph had died and James was now the head of the family and all the sorcerers. He was the head of the Nazarite group and he took Yeshua to Qumran. Here Yeshua spent four years in the celibacy of the Essene community. He learned the individuality of self, the balance of body and spirit, and the worth of energy.

Unlike the Therapeutics Essenes to the south and west, the Qumran Essenes were rigid. They slept but two hours a day. They searched the desert for herbs and roots, but they kept everything they felt within. They were known as "the crazy men." All Judea thought that they were touched with too much sun because of the way they lived. The Essene community at Qumran had been destroyed earlier by an earthquake and they did not live in the structures they had before; they lived in tents and in small units, not in the large buildings which they were slowly repairing. They believed that the earthquake hit because they did not allow a theocratic society to rule Judea, and they took responsibility for that in silence and prayer.

At thirty years of age Yeshua was ready for initiation into the Nazarites, for the rules stated that to be a Nazarite you had to go through thirty years of training in specified areas set down by the head of the order. Thirty years to be a sorcerer, to be a preceptor, to be a healer of people. James was now the head of the order and Yeshua was brought into it. For a period of four and a half years he studied, he worked, he learned, he felt. He travelled with James and the others. They travelled constantly, and the four and a half years progressed and grew to six and then finally to ten years of training as a Nazarite. During this time James saw the power of his brother.

It was now 34 CE and the country was riddled with desertions and battles with the Zealots. John the Baptist had broken away from the Qumran Essene Order and was teaching only two miles from the community itself. The great temple was continuing its sacrificial slaughter of animals. The Judaic faith was strong, as was the school of Hillel, and the Pharisees had great power, though at this time the Sadducees were stronger still.

James called together all of the Nazarites and said that he was stepping down for his brother. Yeshua looked at him and said, "I cannot do it. I cannot teach as a Nazarite. I have other things to do. I see things that need to be done to prepare for the coming of the Messiah. What I learned I have learned well. I have learned from the temple in my younger days. I have learned from the Therapeutic Essenes, from the physician in Damascus. I have learned from Qumran and from the teachings of the celibate cause there. I've learned from the ancient Order of the Nazarites, of the healers, of the physicians, but now I must fence the Torah. I must challenge, for the Messiah is due. He is coming. I feel it. I know it."

Yeshua was a highly intellectual being with great charisma, strength, and power. He was ugly compared to men in your world. He had a mole on his nose and his features were rough and hewn from the sun and the sand. He had lines around his eyes and cheeks, his beard was scraggly and his hair was greasy and never washed. He was unlike the image you might have.

John the Baptist was teaching. The Nazarite community was almost at odds with itself, for they knew that James wanted to step away to follow Yeshua, but at the same time they needed a leader. Yeshua recommended a younger brother of James, and so the younger brother was initiated and became the head of the Nazarites, freeing James to be with Yeshua. After this, Yeshua and James decided to go to Qumran to meditate and review what lay ahead.

In Qumran they were approached by the leader of the community who said to them:

"John is causing great disturbance. He is teaching the teachings of this Essene community to all people. Our secrets, those things that we have guarded for centuries, he is dispersing as he would allow the wind to flow through his hair. It is your duty, Yeshua, to bring his teaching to an end. You must stop it."

So Yeshua and James, with one member of the Qumran community, John, walked to the river. There, John the Baptist was baptizing and preaching the Essene code. He saw them and waved them to come to the water. James, John and Yeshua stepped forward. John the Baptist pushed Yeshua under the water and kept him there until he felt that the spirit had filled him. (Many had lost their lives due to John's leaving them under water until he felt that the spirit had filled them.)

While Yeshua was under the water a great energy took place, a transformation of inner worth. When Yeshua emerged in a transcendental state, John the Baptist said, "I know you. My work is ended. They have sent you to replace me." Yeshua's personality had died there, or that which was his ego of forty years had left his body. He was now a clear passage, a clear channel to an intuitive guidance beyond that which any man had ever had through his disciplines or his perception of self, and John the Baptist knew his work was done. As the Nazarene (from this point onward Yeshua was referred to as "the Nazarene") walked from the water, John the Baptist watched him leave. That evening John the Baptist was arrested by Herod the Second's guards.

The Nazarene went away with his brother James and John to the desert to the south of Qumran. He had heard that John the Baptist had been arrested, and he knew that he had to begin to teach with fervor in order to spread the knowledge throughout Judea. He could no longer just go from person to person and heal. There had to be words and something more. What was it that he was here for? He knew the Law. He knew Deutro Isaiah. He knew the Old Testament. He knew the Pentateuch. He knew the Torah. He had listened to the Zealots and the Essenes. He had seen the confusion of the people in the Temple of the Gentiles. He had seen the power of the Roman soldiers. He had seen the immobility of people. He had seen a nation seething, waiting for the Messiah. Everyone was talking about this coming and had been talking about it for 500 years; each individual thinking it was going to happen on the next day.

The Nazarene began to feel that his energy should be used to walk and teach, as did the Teacher of Righteousness and as Deutro Isaiah had taught; to teach, to give a new insight, to look at the Torah, at the Law, in a new way, to give it a new emphasis and a new way of life. As the inspiration or guidance came forward he knew that he had to show it in a new way. He had to teach it differently from the way it was being taught and to give the people hope and energy in a time of great confusion and chaos due to the imposition of great taxes from the emperor Caligula, imbalances from the Roman head, Pilate, the Zealots, and warring tribes.

The Nazarene remembered that in the Court of the Gentiles in the Temple, there was teacher after teacher who taught the coming of the man who would lead them out of this chaos and they would then rule the world. This was always taught with fear and under great prejudice. The Nazarene knew that it was his time to teach and to approach it from the same way as his father had taught him; to listen, not just to fence, to present in a different way and have his students understand what was being taught.

He remembered the stories his father had taught him. He remembered the stories of the Essenes of Therapeuti, of the stories of the physician of Damascus. He turned to James and said, "Will you go with me? We will not be liked. We'll be called radicals and we'll be one of hundreds of dissidents within Judea." And James agreed, but first he said, "We must gather around us some strong individuals, some companions, some comrades. Come let us go and seek."

The Nazarene found a fisherman named Peter and approached him and said, "Would you come with us? We want to teach a newness." Peter had known him from Qumran, and as he was tired of fishing he gave up his nets. The Nazarene gathered around him seven disciples - not twelve, but seven. Three of the names used as disciples are nicknames for a part of the seven, and so the Bible has some of them mentioned twice, once by a nickname and once by their given name. He gathered them together and said, "It will be hard. We're going to teach in a new way. We will be looked upon in distaste by the Pharisees, by the Sadducees, by the Samaritans, by the Zealots and by the Essenes, but we must step forward." And the work began at the Sea of Tiberius or what is called Galilee. The Nazarene was now forty-one years old. This was in the time of Claudius Caesar when Pontius Pilate ruled Judea and the Nazarene began his teaching.

— CHAPTER FOUR —
THE NAZARENE

The Nazarene was born in 7 BCE and was now 41 years of age in 34 CE. He was different from any other teacher at the time. He would stand in the temple or in a market place and say, "Heed my words. This age is coming to an end. There will be a new day. The cosmic forces are going to arise and the Messiah will appear soon. Get rid of your old ways and put on the new. It is time, it is come, it is the hour—today." If an individual said that on a street corner today, you would think he was either crazy or a fundamentalist. But in Jerusalem it was the rule rather than the exception, for many such teachers, such as the Essenes, taught the same thing. They all had been expecting the Messiah daily. The Essenes of Qumran expected him so strongly that they buried their dead in their clothes so that when he came the dead could rise immediately to greet him.

    The Nazarene was different from any other who had gone before. If he lived today he would be called a promotional artist. He knew how to use words. Consider his training as a sorcerer in the group of sorcerers, his ability to know people, his training with the Essenes or in Damascus, and his knowledge of the ins and outs of the minds of individuals. He did not teach anything that was not already being taught, although he taught it differently. He taught it with gentleness, not with agitation and irritation, but in parables and stories. He took the Torah, the Pentateuch, the Old Testament and taught their essence in small stories, pulling forth their beauty and presenting it for the people to see. This had never been done before.

All of a sudden the scripture came alive with the stories of the Prodigal Son, the Vineyard, the Mustard Seed, the Good Samaritan, and the Prostitute, and the people flocked to hear this person who had the ability to perceive the Law so deeply and understand its intricacies so well that he could use parables and unique stories to emphasize its points. This had never been done before. He said, "Happy are the poor for the kingdom is theirs." This is a direct derivation from the Essene Community which believed the poorer you were and the more you denied yourself, the more in touch with your surroundings you were. "Happy are the gentle for they shall be with God." This comes directly from the 37th Psalm. "Happy are those that mourn for they will be comforted." This is a direct quote from the 126th Psalm. "Happy are those who seek relief in righteousness for they will be guarded or relieved." This is direct from Proverbs. "Happy are the merciful for they will have mercy." This came directly from Samuel.

The Sermon on the Mount was actually direct quotations from the Old Testament. There was no Sermon on the Mount. It was only a conglomeration of talks here and there, pulled together as one unit by the New Testament writers so that they could present a powerful package. The Nazarene taught his thoughts and feelings far and wide, and as the New Testament authors began to write they combined everything and said, "We will put all of this together to make it strong and emphatic."

The basis of his new teaching was as he said, "The teaching, 'love thy neighbor and hate your enemy' must be replaced with 'love your enemy as you love thy neighbor.'" This teaching was new to the Judaic faith. The Essene Community taught love your friends and your comrades, but hate your enemies. This was a whole new approach and the nucleus of his teachings. "First love your God and then, second, love yourself and your neighbor." This was directly from the Pentateuch, from Leviticus and from Deuteronomy. The only new teaching from the Nazarene was "Love your enemy" and no other. All the rest was direct quotations from the Old Testament for he knew it inside and out.

The Nazarene taught all his disciples, but he gathered close around him only three; his brother, James, John, and Peter, and they became an intimate group. He began to share with them knowledge which he did not teach regularly. He began to teach them the wisdom of the Torah, the wisdom of Judaism, but even beyond these with a string of knowledge that went beyond Moses and the Pharaohs. "Bring Life to the Inner Spirit."

The Nazarene and the three would withdraw to the mountain where he initiated the three and worked with them individually. They became an inseparable triumvirate. They were his power and his strength during his teaching. He could perform miracles because he was a sorcerer and knew how to heal. He was an excellent healer; he could walk up to a person, look him in the eye, and cure him simply by knowing what was wrong. He had the ability to talk to an individual and pull the evil spirits out of them. The use of herbs and positive projection, to engender the faith in an individual to believe in himself, enabled him to heal on the spot.

And so, unlike any other teacher before that time, the Nazarene taught not only in a new way but also with the power of an excellent healer and would casually work with those who came to him. He did not seek great renown. He was tested by the Pharisees and the Sadducees but would always throw back the Torah, the Pentateuch, and the ancient scriptures, so that there was no way they could say that what he was doing was wrong, but rather that he had a "wisdom."

The Nazarene was a unique individual for the time. He had an unobstructed connection to his Higher Self. He had the knowledge and the power of a healer and had the ability to teach and to make people believe in themselves.

The Nazarene knew people and he knew them well. He calmed the waters and walked upon them. That is not difficult; anyone who knows the elements and the essence of atoms and molecules has the ability to walk on water. To be able to identify himself with that liquid and see it as a hard substance was no great feat of calming. But the story of the boat and the water, that was not an actuality. It was a parable, again misconstrued by the New Testament writers. (The individual was the boat, the water was the outside world, and the Nazarene was the inner self, the soul.) He calmed the waters by standing up and taking prominence within the boat. So, the waters, the permanent waters of your world, can be calmed by the source standing up within you and calming things around you. But the New Testament writers and future Christians were so anxious to shock and bring about new, exciting, and different occurrences that they looked under rocks, behind trees, and in holes for anything that would seem unusual. There was an unusualness here, but it was consistent with the times and the social climate.

Pontius Pilate, a strong and greatly intelligent man, was on the Judean throne and resided in his Caesarean palace. When he took office he sent his roman soldiers, with all the symbols of their gods, into Jerusalem. There was such a great gnashing of teeth by the Sanhedrin that Pilate had to take away the posts, because the Sanhedrin threw themselves before the soldiers and said "You will have to kill us all if the temple is to have these pagan gods of your army." Pilate took money from the temple to build an aqueduct from Caesarea to Jerusalem. He defied the authority of the Sadducee party every time he could.

The Zealots were constantly killing Jews who co-operated with Pilate. There was much turmoil and there were many single individuals who were teaching insurrection. Jerusalem was in turmoil. Only 30 years after this time, the Roman empire had the only internal uprising it ever had, and it was in Jerusalem. That was the only internal war of the empire that ever faced Rome and it was boiling and bubbling at this time.

Pilate's spies were everywhere. He listened to information about anyone especially any rumors about the coming Messiah. However, soon the soldiers took it as if someone were saying "good morning" when they heard "the Messiah is coming." There are current faiths within your world who believe every ten years that the Messiah is coming but then have to postpone it when he does not arrive.

The Nazarene taught around the Sea of Tiberius, now known as the Sea of Galilee. He did not go into large cities and he taught only Jews, even though more than 50% of the population of Judea was foreign. He listened and talked while he walked. He honored the Pharisees, the Torah, and the scriptures, for he taught from them. He did not deny them; they were his sources. He strongly stated, "It is the Law that will stand always," and the Torah was the Law.

The Nazarene was a strong individual with good training who knew his scripture. His training was good. He had gone through the best teaching of the time and gathered around him seven disciples: seven individuals who supported and learned from him, helped him, and brought him food and drink.

Lazarus was actually John, one of the three: James, John, and Peter. John was told that he was dying and he knew it. He was buried but three days later he arose. He was initiated, as were James and Peter, in the release and surrender of both their inner self and their outer self.

The Nazarene was constantly withdrawing to rebuild, to review his work and the parables of his teachings, such as the parable of the Good Samaritan. The Good Samaritan is the story of a wounded individual who lay by the roadside and was passed by a Pharisee who would not help him, but who was then aided by a Samaritan. During that period of time this would be like someone now saying "and a good KKK member healed him," for the Samaritans were looked on with disfavor. The Nazarene drove home points of law through stories, whether it was the Vineyard and the Mustard Seed, or the Good Samaritan. He was a teacher. He knew how to present himself and how to show the law so his listeners would understand.

The Nazarene had been training James, John and Peter within an ancient wisdom; a teaching that he taught no one else. There were four other strong disciples that were around him. There were also many women who were perceiving and listening. He gathered together, on a Friday evening, these seven for the Seder meal and they broke bread and drank wine together. As the Essene community would say, "This is the bread, it is the body, instead of the sacrificial lamb." And they drank wine and said "This is the wine, instead of the blood." It was not Passover for if it had been Passover the whole family would have been together. Before he left he turned to his disciple Judas and said, "You will deliver a great service," and Judas did not know what he meant.

He told them that he must go into Jerusalem into the Court of Gentiles and teach. He had prepared for this. Through his teaching in communities around the Sea of Tiberius he had learned how to present and pull people to him. He asked James, John and Peter to remain back while he took the others with him to Jerusalem.

The Nazarene went into the temple and began to teach in the Court of the Gentiles. People were drawn to his magnetism, to his charisma, to the fact that he could look at a being, see what was wrong, and feel their energy. People would come and feel the life force within themselves, the rejuvenation of the enzymes, of the hormones within their body. He said, <u>"I am the Messiah, I am the Christ."</u> He taught that within you, you would find the Father, or the God. Nothing that the Nazarene said was wrong, even though he said he was the Christ, the Messiah; even though he said he had come to lead everyone away, even though he said he had come to teach and preach the scripture and to lead everyone to a new world. There were hundreds within the Court of

Gentiles who had been saying that for years, so he committed no blasphemy. He did not claim to be Yahweh, which would have been blasphemy. He said he was the son of God, but within the temple all would have been sons of God, of Yahweh, and that was not unusual.

An inquiry was made in the temple by some of the priests. They asked the Nazarene who he was and he told them. They asked, "Are you the Christ or do you say you are?" and he said, "Yes I am, but so are you." This was not against their Law. He did not blaspheme, for had he blasphemed, all of the council, all the Sadducees would have rent their clothes and gnashed their teeth, not just the High Priests.

The money changers were making a lot of noise, asking for customers and calling out the new prices as the Nazarene was teaching his parables. The money changers were so loud that he could hardly hear what he was saying and he yelled, "Quiet." And there was silence. As he began to teach again the money changers did not like it so they called the temple guards. Although the guards came, looked, and listened, they could not find him until the money changers said "There he is." He was arrested and placed in the prison of the temple.

The Sadducees attempted to keep Pilate in line by appeasing him and from time to time they would hand over a political or religious figure to him so that he would feel that they were on his side. It was just such a time as Pilate had had much difficulty. The Zealots had recently killed many Romans and he was feeling a need to do some persecution to set an example. The priests knew that if the Nazarene got in front of Pilate and said he was the Messiah, the Deliverer, Pilate would feel that he got a revolutionary and the Nazarene would be killed.

Judas (Judas Iscariot means Judas the Deliverer) had been one of the four who had gone with the Nazarene to the temple. He saw what happened and ran back, trying to find James, John, and Peter. He could not find them so he hurried into the city hoping that he would be able to intercede, but he could not. Then he remembered that James, John, and Peter had a place high in the hills where they went to meditate. and that was probably where the three had gone to send energy to the Nazarene. He found them and told them what had happened. They sent him back and said, "Try to get him released. He must be gotten out of prison. It cannot end here, for if he goes before Pilate he surely will either be stoned or hung from the cross."

Meanwhile, the Nazarene did appear before Pilate. He had been teaching only one year and he faced Pilate. Pilate asked "What wrong have you done?" and the Nazarene said, *"No wrong."* "Who are you?" *"I am Yeshua."* "What do you teach? Why were you sent here?" *"They said I had done wrong in the temple, that I am the Messiah,"* and Pilate's ears perked up thinking the Nazarene was a rebel; one of those many small groups that was causing so much terror and difficulty. "Do you say that you are the Messiah, this Deliverer that everyone is looking for?" *"I am from within."* said the Nazarene, and that he was the Messiah, that he was the one who came to deliver, to give the word, to help individuals go beyond their personal view of the Torah or the scriptures. Pilate said, "Then you will die. But first you must be placed within the prison. You must be placed upon the rack. You must be whipped and beaten," for this was the procedure for those who were to be hung on the cross so that they would not survive for long periods of time. The Nazarene had to go through the scourge, through the beating, for that would tone him down and hasten his death upon the hill with the other criminals.

Meanwhile, Pilate had put out an order that a man named Barabbas had to be captured. He was a rebel and he was killing. He was responsible for many robberies. His full name was Yeshua Barabbas. Yeshua Barabbas was caught and taken to the Roman dungeons and there he was imprisoned.

It was not Passover, it was not Easter. It was just another weekend.

The Nazarene was thrown into prison and Pilate thought he had done well. But just at this time he had received word that Claudius Caesar had appointed him to a grand new position in the Senate at Rome, so in celebration he said, "I will release one prisoner. I'll show you how great I am. I will release this eccentric Yeshua" and he passed this message to the guards. The guards were unsure which prisoner to release. Pilate had said to release Yeshua, the one that he had committed a while ago. They went down into the dungeons and they came to a cell asking, "Are you Yeshua?" Barabbas said, "Yes." The guards, not being of the best of mental faculties, released Yeshua Barabbas. Barabbas was a thief, a robber, a murderer, a rapist, and was more involved in the "evil ways" against Rome than the Nazarene, who was a healer and a teacher

That night Judas went to the guard in the prison and said, "I have a sack of money. I will give you this sack of gold talents if you will let me take my prisoner out." And the guard said, "It is done." But first, said Judas, "You will have to drug him with this potion or else he will not go. Put this in his evening wine." And then the guard said, "I will put it in the food but I will not be there and you must come and get him." And so Judas came and took away the Nazarene. As the Nazarene slept, Judas carried him over his shoulder and was met at the gate by James, John and Peter, who then took the Nazarene and escaped Jerusalem. They went to Qumran and then further away into the wilderness. The Nazarene was still drugged and asleep.

The guard returned and when he saw that the Nazarene was gone he felt happy. Then came a Tribune who said "Prepare the prisoner for scourging and for beating. Pilate wants this one done well." The fearful guard went out searching for someone the same size as the Nazarene. He found a replacement and beat him, cut him, and drugged him. He placed a crown upon his head as was done in those times. The substituted prisoner could not carry his cross because he was drugged. Peter had returned to see what was happening and when he saw the Nazarene's substitute he denied that it was Yeshua. Judas also returned for the same reasons. The drugged substitute was hung upon the cross and he muttered words that every Jew knew from the Psalms and that every Jew with pain and misery would mumble, much as you would mumble. "God help me," and then he died. The guard tore him down and burned his body but realizing that Judas knew of this, sought out Judas and murdered him. The guard was not aware of Peter, James, and John. All evidence was lost and the guard was free. Peter returned to James, John, and the Nazarene in the wilderness and told them of what had transpired and that people had not paid any attention. No one came to visit the cross; it was just another execution.

Now, the Nazarene wondered what he was to do. He was officially dead; if he returned he would surely be looked upon as a god. People would think that he had returned from the dead. He spoke to James, John, and Peter about this. James, called "James the Just," knew this could not be the way. The Nazarene knew that his work, his teachings, were at an end and so he withdrew with James, John, and Peter to the deep desert of Jordan. In Jordan he finished the training of his three disciples using what he had learned over long years of study and what he had learned through the God Force.

The key to his teaching of the three was to pass to them the teachings of the Torah with parables, love, and kindness and not with fear as others were doing. He taught them as he had learned with the Essene colony of Qumran. He wanted them to continue to teach but only to those who were drawn to them and who could keep silent. *"You will be sought after. People will want to know what it was like being with me."* The Nazarene taught them of the wisdoms that he had learned in Egypt. He taught them of the physician's teachings that had come from the hermetic and Horace. The Nazarene had the connection to his Higher Self, he had the way, and he had the energy within him. But he knew that if he returned it would be a farce and would cause such difficulty to the people that the only and best way was to stop now and hope that these three individuals would be able to carry the message silently and have it continued throughout history. He wanted them to keep the power and the beauty of scripture; that of the suffering servant, and of the Teacher of Righteousness, so that both men and women would have hope.

For a long period of six months he taught James, John, and Peter. It was evening and the sun was fading over the hills. The four had been camped upon the top of a hill for all this time. The Nazarene felt that his work was done, but he was unsure what to do next, as he was confused in one way but released in another. A Jew first, but also a man of vision, of Essene communication, and of the world, he walked to the edge of a cliff and spread his arms wide in the form of a cross, and with pain and with tears said, *"Help me Yahweh."* No one had mentioned or muttered Yahweh's name except the head priest in 500 years.

In a flash of light he was cremated by lightning. Why? Things are purified by fire. He knew speaking the powerful word "Yahweh" out loud was a sacrilege but it also was a release for him from the world. He knew that speaking the name in Jerusalem he would have been stoned, but if he did it here in order to be released, he would be and released he was.

James, John, and Peter were horrified, stunned, and confused. They could not go back and say, "Yeshua really died by a lightning bolt." They could not go back and say, "We stole him from the prison and he died outside some place." What they knew was theirs and theirs alone and they must keep it that way. They returned to Jerusalem and worshiped in the temple, as did all the other disciples. They did not leave the temple. They still sacrificed the lambs. But James, John, and Peter began to feel the need for movement. They began to travel and teach what the Nazarene had taught and people would come to them and say, "Tell us of the Nazarene," and they would tell them.

Meanwhile, in Jerusalem a great turmoil was beginning. As these three began to find strength within their belief and within their mutual secret, the other followers of the Nazarene started a small community and lived together. This community was not large compared to the Essenes or the Zealots, but they communicated back and forth and believed in the teachings of the Nazarene. The Nazarene had looked back to the Psalms which stated, "He who comes or that will be subjected and pushed down, will die for your sins." This was intended for Israel, not for the Nazarene. But they took this as their belief.

Myths began to develop about him. Followers of the Nazarene began to tell stories and enlarged upon what he did. Instead of talking to ten it was a hundred. Instead of walking four miles it was four hundred. The followers began to increase and pull other individuals to tell them about their teacher, about the individual who believed so strongly that he was willing to die for what he believed. But not once did they say he was God. Not once did they say he was Yahweh. And the small group began to grow.

The appeal was the fact that they brought in women; that they would allow women to join. None of the others allowed women; Essenes of Qumran—no women, Zealots—no women, Judaism in its finest form—no women within the temple. Women liked that inclusion and they became the strength and the nucleus. The followers of the Nazarene began to understand that if you don't know anything about someone you can create a stronger belief in them than if you know everything about them. And so, because his life was not written down, because the ending was so confusing, and his life was short, belief was strong.

Buddha had taught for 40 years and had a large group of disciples who had learned his message, while the Nazarene taught for only one year. Those around the Nazarene had to search for memories that were then passed by word of mouth, as there was still no writing.

In the year after the Nazarene's death, the same year that Pontius Pilate had to return to Rome because of misuse of power within Judea, a man by the name of Paul was on his way to Damascus. Paul was a small man, five foot one, balding, uglier than Yeshua. He had a thorn that he carried with him for he had a skin disease that smelled and that he was constantly itching, to the chagrin of others. He was a triple fire element and was hard to be around. If he did not like something he would not say he did not like it, he would say, "Get rid of it."

It was the year 36 CE and Paul had a vision. But Paul had lots of visions; he had had visions from birth. He believed that he was anointed within his mother's womb to bring forth great teachings and to do great things in the world. He was a part of the Judaic faith, a part of the temple that believed in communicating with the dead beyond. He believed in psychic phenomena, so to speak; in fact, there was a part of the Pharisee group that believed there were seven heavens and that you could enter them and have experiences in them through meditation. Paul himself had said that he had gone as high as four.

On the road to Damascus, the Nazarene appears to him or perhaps an energy appears to him. He sees the energy, the power, the beauty and it tells him that he must go and teach…and what does he do? He meditates on what he has seen. He withdraws to the same area that Peter, James, and John had taken the Nazarene. He withdrew; he did not run to Jerusalem to seek out other Christians. He had never seen the Nazarene, never heard of him. Who was he? There he began to build his visionary force. In fact, he did not meet any of the disciples or anyone connected to the Nazarene for three years after this vision, and he continued to teach in the synagogue.

As Paul began to travel and write he did not go to a forum, he went to the synagogue. He was first a Jew, and never did he say that Yeshua was God. He always said it was through the temple and through understanding that the Nazarene came to deliver individuals from the monotony, from the chaos of the Torah and the adherents to the Law. But first was the Judaic code, and he always talked in the temple. In all of his life he never once mentioned the miracles nor the parables told by the Nazarene. He did not even consider in any of his writings the way the Nazarene had died, (but he thought that was a terrible way to go; which was true).

Paul taught directly from the scripture, from the Old Testament: woman has her place, daughter has her place. He did not mention those elements of the Sermon on the Mount, because there was no Sermon on the Mount. He did not teach the basic teaching that the Nazarene came forward with that was: *"Love your neighbor and Love your enemy."* Paul was a dynamic little man. He would have made millions for any company he would have worked for. He believed that he was on a mission and that he had the source.

Did the Nazarene really appear to Paul? Why the Nazarene and not another one of the many individuals who were teaching? At this time, the Nazarene had been gone for six months. Paul's vision came at the same time the Nazarene had left his body in a pile of dust. Within your world when people begin to leave their bodies they are sometimes seen in bedrooms and in places across the world or all of a sudden you get a feeling of them. If all of a sudden, someone stood in front of you, you might say, "What do you want? Do you want me to teach? All right, I'll teach," and you didn't have to say anything at all. Due to Paul's vision and his identification with it, and because of his energy and power at the time, this is what Paul experienced.

Paul traveled the Mediterranean world four times. He taught in every synagogue that was there until they threw him out. But he found one interesting thing; that within each synagogue was a group of people called "The God Fearers." These were the individuals who were brought to the synagogue but were not Jews. They were looking for some identification. They could not be Jews, but they liked the messages, the power, and the consistency of the one God, of the Torah, and the Judaic faith. It was these people who began to ask Paul for letters. It was these people who began to come to him. It was these individuals who began to find a power within, and Paul began to teach them. These individuals became the Christians.

Paul was not a Christian. He was a Jew and he died a Jew. This small man travelled and wrote constantly. He was a powerhouse. He founded Christianity.

What Paul put together and the way he taught was all based on one thing—the Old Testament, the Torah, and the Pentateuch, and the fact that the Nazarene came and had been with God and knew him. And it was through understanding what the Nazarene was teaching that one would know Yahweh. Paul said the Nazarene would return with the power from God, from Yahweh—(not actually mentioning Yahweh of course). He will return with the power and lead us out of this situation of Roman control. Paul, right to the last moment, to his last breath, thought the Nazarene was returning; the Messiah was returning, as did hundreds and hundreds of Jews.

In 66 CE Jerusalem revolted and Rome had one of the most difficult wars it had ever had. Hundreds of thousands were killed. The temple of gold and beauty and strength was brought to the ground and the Emperor declared that it was to become dust. Every brick was beaten to dust. Everything within it was taken away. Nothing was left. The devout held out at the very end in Massabec, high upon the mountain, and slowly they were starved to death by the Roman armies. The last 900 drew lots; nine of those killed the remainder of the 900, one killed the eight and then killed himself. At that, the Sadducee Party ended. There was no temple and all the priests of the temple and most of the Levites were dead. Judaism had been pushed to the very ends.

And Paul was teaching, "Follow the Nazarene. It is through him you will find Yahweh. Be prepared for the coming. It will be like fire from heaven." A demented ruler in Rome heard that statement and said "The Christians caused Rome to burn, they sent fire from heaven," and it was the first time that the Christians were persecuted, killed by the hundreds. Paul was not killed then. He was later caught, tried, and executed. He died from the great difficulty of trying to keep his head connected to his body. He was a Roman citizen because his mother and father were wealthy

Jews of Damascus of Tarsus. He had Roman citizenship, so when he was caught and tried he was able to have his head chopped off, as any good Roman citizen could, rather than being stoned or hung from a cross. His severed head hung from a pole in a center square for thirteen years, which wasn't long compared to some others.

What of James, John, and Peter? Forget what you have heard of Peter. Peter was not the patriarch of the church any more than you are. He was a powerful man. He was strong and he had energy and he was a part of the nucleus. James the Just, Yeshua's brother, died of arthritis. It was said he died because he was on his knees all the time and when he couldn't get up one day, he died of hunger while still in a kneeling position. John too, died a natural death. Peter, fearing that his knowledge of the Nazarene and what they had learned would be forgotten, wrote it down in a series of four transcripts. Just before his death he befriended an individual who had become a Christian named Barnabas, and he passed the scrolls on to him. Barnabas went to Rome, and it was through Barnabas that the Catholic Church was developed.

Barnabas passed these documents on to two or three others. They kept the secret, but one of them became Pope. Those documents are still in the Vatican deep within its chambers. The knowledge of them is there but hidden and sealed under the archives. The small group led by James, John, and Peter grew in silence. They were known eventually as the Cathars and the Altingenese. They were the Gnostics. But there were always the few who knew more than the rest on the periphery of those Gnostics.

To this day, there is a small group that has a connection and knows each individual part of the story that you are reading now. That does not mean that it needs to be a secret, for you are beyond that. But if it were revealed within the Catholic Church, what would the Church have? Nothing; nothing from all those years of developing and bringing the sacraments and all, from the death of Paul until now. Paul died a Jew just as John Wesley died an Episcopal, not a Methodist, and Martin Luther died a Catholic, not a Lutheran. Paul was first a Jew but he created Christianity with the "Godfearers." Those early Christians were persecuted; hung from crosses, eaten by lions, because they believed at the last moment, the messiah was going to come and help them, and deliver them from that cross.

The Jews who died in Massabec, the 900, each thought, to the last second, that the Messiah was going to come and ruin the Roman army. Therefore, in the time of Nero and death of Paul, the Jewish faith was on its knees, Christians had been martyred, and women were accepted. That was the key and that is what made Christianity what it is today, the complete acceptance of women within it. Whereas Judaism didn't. Men and women were separated. Buddhism didn't, and Nephryism didn't. Nephryism was the god of the Roman soldiers. The gods of Rome were masculine and the feminine gods could only be worshipped by the rulers.

As the women began to achieve what they had always hoped, the organization began to grow. Women, from that time until now, have always been the greatest believers, and they began to find hope in something they could not see. Women are always the ones that have the greatest faith; Their belief is stronger than men will ever have. As the small community began to come together and develop, from 60 CE to 110 CE, they needed the written word. They needed to talk and record what the Nazarene was. Paul was dead, Peter was dead, James and John were dead, and all the other disciples were dead. And so they began to write what they had heard, felt, and seen, some of it second—third—and fourth—hand. Although Paul had never seen the Nazarene, his letters were all intact. It took until 300 CE to complete the New Testament.

There were many individual letters and writers. In fact, the writers Matthew, Mark and Luke were so embarrassed about writing they adopted pseudonyms for they did not want people to know they were the authors. There were no actual lies in the gospels; if there were lies and direct misrepresentations, they would have been more blatant. The writers were so new to the game that they blundered through.

The writers could have easily made the Nazarene die at the Passover. Would the USA kill a man on Christmas Day by execution? Can you imagine on the highest festival that all the police would get together to rule over one little person that no one had heard of? On the Passover you got together with the women also, not just the men. There were too many inconsistencies. The basic truth is contained in what the Nazarene directly said; disregard what is reported that he said, where he went, or what had been done (for example walking on the water, feeding of thousands, and teaching to the multitudes.) He did teach, but not necessarily to hundreds and hundreds or the multitudes. It sounded better if he taught to hundreds and hundreds, and that multitudes attended.

As they began to compile these writings, being Jews first, they pulled from the Old Testament of Isaiah and also from the Psalms, which says "He died for our sins" and "He died of being pierced of the hands and feet." These sayings were for Israel but these verses were applied specifically to the Nazarene and inserted into the New Testament. It was interesting that at one time a small group of Jews were going to the Old Testament pulling out things to place within a New Testament and that today there are small groups that go to the New Testament to pull out things.

This process is unending but it is the key. To start a major religion or a major power within your world, you must have four things. First, you must have a charismatic leader who is teaching something that is old and that thousands believe in, but teaching it in a new and different way. Secondly, you need a good publicity expert, like Paul. Third, you must include women, and fourth, the leader should be relatively unknown so that his past and his accomplishments can be embellished or reconstructed. Those are the four catalysts to creating a world religion: a power, a strength, a beauty. They have all been created for naught. Is it all a sham? Is it all nothing now, the sanctuaries, the crusades, the martyrs, the saints?

— CHAPTER FIVE —

QUESTIONS

Throughout history, nations have constantly changed: men fighting over a cause; councils meeting and determining what was right and wrong; and churches, priests, and popes deciding that Jesus was God, making Mary elite, creating fundamental law that had no scriptural beginning, interpreting where interpretation was a thin veil. People who believed deeply were persecuted. There were many levels of purgatory created and you had to pay penance because you did something wrong. Centuries roll by, crusades where young children lost their lives marching to free Jerusalem of the heathens, of nation against nation who believed in the same Christian God, of religion fighting religion, of man and woman unable to marry because one believed that you shouldn't wear lipstick and another that you could, of religions constantly fighting one another but all saying that Jesus was the center. Churches were built with emblems—symbols of a cross that he never hung upon. Pictures of individuals that other individuals felt were important for their strong energy.

Money has been spent in every area to bring opulence to religion with priests, nuns, and ministers. There have been Christian kings and queens misusing each and every thing, and not following the only teaching that the Nazarene taught that was different; "Love your neighbor, love your enemy." The Nazarene only taught one thing that was different than the whole Judaic Law and that is the only thing they did not follow. Man must learn and he learns the hard way. The Nazarene said, "It is within that you will find the kingdom."

Why did the Nazarene not go back to Jerusalem to give himself up and tell what had happened? Would he not have been better off? Would it have stopped the chaos that the centuries have created? One always reacts by doing what he thinks is the best for the moment and hoping that it will be best for the future. You must always know that no one is responsible for you, aside from yourself.

Were Moses, the Jews, Judah and Yeshua all of the same race and if so what was that race?

Starting with Abraham there were tribes like the Native Americans which were nomadic and always moving around. There were 12 basic tribes. These tribes had no religion or creed, but they had traditions. There were also other tribes in what is now called Algeria, Iran, Iraq, and Saudi Arabia that crossed into Judea and lived in the same area. They sometimes came together to celebrate certain festivals. The Pharaoh saw these tribes as a threat and came out of Egypt to capture them and make them slaves.

The various tribes were captured to be slaves within Egypt. The slaves that escaped with Moses were part of this same group. At that time they were not Jewish, they were just tribesmen who were slaves. The tribes had come together only because they had been enslaved and Moses freed them. There was not a Jewish nation until 537 BCE, after the exile from Babylon. Even though Judea was created during the time of David, it was not Jewish. There were still tribal gods and much tribal warfare. Yahweh was still centered through one major priest whether it was Samuel, Nathan, Elijah, or Elisha. The Torah was not yet a major force.

The Ark of the Covenant, which was supposed to have carried some of the original elements and trinkets, was used as a powerful force, but it was a mostly a symbol. The Jewish nation was not created until the exile and then it became a written religion with a secular organization.

Did Mary have any more children?

First, Joseph was quite old when he conceived Yeshua. After Yeshua was born, Mary cared for Yeshua while traveling. Joseph taught Yeshua as much as he could until he was 12 years old. Mary had another child when Yeshua was approximately nine years old and that child, Gamaliel, became a major part of the Judaic faith, becoming a Sadducee. He was reported to be the son of Helia, which was not true. Helia had only daughters. Gamaliel was killed in 68 CE by the Romans. Yeshua's older brothers were from a different mother.

Was Mary still alive when Yeshua died?

Yes, Mary was alive but not involved. Since Yeshua did not follow the ways of the Sorcerers of the Nazarites, his family, except his brother James the Just, did not think much of Yeshua. In fact, they felt he was an outcast until the very end. At that point they began to understand what he was doing and were somewhat supportive, but it was not until the very last part of Yeshua's life.

Millions of people in our world believe Yeshua is coming back some day. What do you think? Is that feasible?

There are Jews who think the Messiah is coming to deliver them and to help them against the Arab world. They entered the Seven Day War thinking that the Messiah would be on their side and help lead them out of the situation they are in. There are those who thought, as Paul thought, that the Nazarene would return and Yeshua would come back. Time and time again it has been the hope. Why should he come back? If he came back it would only be to aid those who needed something outside of themselves, and they would never know he was here. They would go on with their daily lives. Yeshua, per se, will not return. It is not needed and the world energy is at a state where it will not happen in this cataclysmic period.

Chung Fu, was there a specific female energy that supported Yeshua any time during his life here?

You must understand that this individual was unique. Through his training and his energy, he learned to channel the positiveness into a perfect connection of the positive and negative within. He did not need the female as a balance. But he was also the first spiritual teacher to draw women to him because they felt the balance of His energy and were comfortable around it.

You mentioned that the Egyptians took members of the Twelve Tribes to Egypt as slaves. Could you explain what happened to those who were not taken and managed to escape?

Some of them went deep into the African continent, becoming part of the traditions of the Urubu, Ashanti, Bulu, Ebanome and Alanti. They settled within the Gold Coast or Upper Volta area, within the Congo and Uganda and within the west coast of Tanzania. Another group went into the high mountains of the Iranian area and became the nomadic tribes that moved freely and still do today within that country

Is there a significance to Yeshua being born under a tree rather than in a manger or in a house?

The significance seems to follow a pattern: Buddha was born under a tree, Lao Tzu was born under a tree, and Zoroaster was born under a tree and died under a tree. The tree has been the symbol of life. And Yeshua, at the end, had his feet to the earth and arms spread to the world, as a tree does. The tree symbolizes acceptance of all and completeness. It has always accepted anything that comes within its branches and shelters and gives fruit. It has its roots deep in the earth. It fertilizes. It is one of the oldest living units within your planet. It is a symbol of nature.

What time of year was Yeshua born?

Mid-October.

How did Palm Sunday come about?

It was said that the Nazarene entered Jerusalem with palms before him one week prior to the time he was crucified. This comes from Isaiah as a direct quote. The writers of Matthew, Mark, Luke, and John drew from the Old Testament as much as they could. They had no way of knowing how Yeshua went into Jerusalem and so they did it this way. If Yeshua was to be what they thought Isaiah was talking about in the "suffering servant," then this was the way he would have had to come in. And so if he was to be the Messiah, then he would have to follow what Isaiah or Deutro Isaiah had said would happen. It was not necessarily a flagrant lie, it was just that they did not know.

They arrive at this through deduction. If you wondered how an individual finished a math problem and got a specific answer, and if you knew that it was passed on from the original law, you would go back to the original law and you would say, "They did it this way to get that answer to the problem." You would not necessarily feel that they cheated or looked over someone's shoulder. It was a natural deduction, but it also makes one realize that much of what is written in regard to movement, location, and content in those four gospels has very little reliability. Yeshua's actual words are higher in reliability. Most everything else that was placed there had "scriptural reference" to the Old Testament or was placed there to entice individuals to be part of it.

The star at Yeshua's birth was a reality but the early writers did not quite understand what it meant because these were Jews who were not necessarily steeped within the Essene or the Zoroastrian culture, and they did not know the alignment it signified. They had heard that the Zoroastrians did and so they included this hoping that this would also pull some Zoroastrian individuals into Christianity. Much of Matthew, Mark, and Luke were what you may call "putting things together" to make it more palatable. It is somewhat like putting sorbitol over a B vitamin complex to make it easier to take.

Were Mary and Yeshua dual mates and did he reincarnate out?

Mary was not. Yeshua was not what you would call a dual mate. He was an individual who had completed his cycle through Zoroaster and returned to give an energy influx to the world and breadth with a new teaching. Jewish capitalism was to shape the future of the United States and the Western World. The Jews, through their ways and forcefulness, along with the Judaic-Christians, created the capitalistic society. The Nazarene came to divert that and to create an energy force at the most crucial time that the world has seen in the last 7,000 years. It was the seep of history. There wasn't anything going on in China. There wasn't much going on in the Mayan or the Andean civilizations; they were strong and solid. It was only within this part of the world that the great energy, the great battles, the great divergences, were occurring and so an energy was sent to allow two nuclei to come together.

Old Chinese, was Yeshua the only one to lose or send back his ego and operate only from the Higher Self? Was this part of the plan? Why was he the only one?

No, it is not correct that Yeshua was the only one to lose his ego or his subconscious mind although he was one who did. He returned after finishing his cycle in the earth plane and worked with regards to that completion. There have been others who have done the same thing. We will attempt to explain about plan, predestination, or probability.

We will give you an example about Old Chinese. Those who teach Old Chinese have said that for him to connect within your world and to work within the physical plane, you have to keep a level of energy vibration of one million cycles per second. We don't care how you keep that energy. It is a positive energy, but you keep it. You must do anything that you can, but it has to be positive for if it is negative it will drop below that one million cycle per second. So, Old Chinese has the leeway of working with people, with individuals, but always to increase or keep that energy in a particular position.

In a previous cataclysm there was an individual like Yeshua known as Zeus. Now this was a different cycle; it was not the same time. It was a little later, for that cycle was twelve thousand years instead of seven thousand; it averages seven thousand. Yeshua's coming into the earth plane was an energy input. In the beginning of a cyclic period, there needs to be energy inputs; like getting gasoline for your automobile, or feeding your body. This cycle, this phase of energy, needs those inputs. Lao Tzu and Confucius were inputs. Yeshua was an input; a major overhaul in energy. The time of the great magicians in the 1700's and 1800's were an input. The time of the great artist in the 1400's and 1500's were an input. The time of the great energy of the Chinese poets were an input. The time of the great creativity of the Mayan civilization was an input. These fed the energy that your world needs to keep moving.

Old Chinese knows that he must keep the energy at one-million-cycles per second, for if he goes below that, his work finishes and he must withdraw and no longer teach. He has been assigned this one-million-cycle per second energy as a part of the total energy in order to keep this cycle going. If he pulls back, it creates a domino effect and someone else has to make it up. If they are unable to then they have to withdraw. If you have many withdrawals you have sudden changes in the earth plane, and you find yourself swimming very fast or moving within great movements.

Chung Fu, do you think where Yeshua was born they are going to have peace in our time?

Let us put it this way: Israel is like England and is not happy if they are not at war. It is a part of their whole character. They believed, in the beginning, that they were the chosen people and that they would do anything to rule the world. They have been constantly persecuted since. Their thoughts and feelings are an energy. It is from this energy that movement occurs. There will not be peace there. There will constantly be war, as it has been a warring place for thousands of years.

The island of England also has been a warring island for thousands of years. Since before the time of the Vikings there has been battle upon battle. When there's peace, they are miserable because there is no activity, no energy. Many peaceful nations still have an energy for they create it within their own society and creative work. Within the Americas there is no need for war because you are creating constantly new energy, new thoughts, new buildings, new places. Within the English part of the world, tradition and heritage hold on and do not allow tearing down and rebuilding, so it is stale. No, there will not be peace in the Middle East.

Old Chinese, after the next cataclysm, when people are sitting around telling their children about Yeshua, what will they say?

They will probably say the same as those that sat around and told about Zeus. Think of what is told about Zeus now. He raped every goddess that he could find and any other human female available. The story was misused. Let us say, as an analogy, that you are nine or ten years old and this story is being told to you. There was this man who lived and taught the Law. He taught peace and beauty and strength. He taught all the things that Yeshua taught and that you should remember. And you say "Why should I remember? There was still a cataclysm and I am here with nothing. Why should I remember that?" "Because it is beautiful." "How is it beautiful?" "It is beautiful to learn, to know those things that have been." And your children have children and they say, "My mother and father told me this story about this man…" And so it goes. Along the way it gets blown out of proportion or it is not as strong or emphatic and cannot create that spark again. This is part of the cycle; a part of the existences upon this earth plane.

Chung Fu, is there anything to be gained through prayer to Yeshua?

Prayer is an outpouring of those things that are within you. Anything that is expressed by the individual as, "I need help," or "This is what I need" is good. Yeshua is a symbol, an energy, and if you can learn by saying, "Yeshua help me" it is the same as saying "Help myself." The answer is "Yes," for it at least gets you to conversing within and allowing this to come forth, allowing the energy to project and enabling you to examine it. When you examine it, then you can begin to work with the inner force that will come through silence.

Chung Fu, is the Quran in the Bible part of the same Quran?

Yes

Who is the Yeshua energy in the Quran?

The Yeshua energy in the Quran developed basically out of Babylon. The Quran's main force developed there and the Yeshua energy is what you would call the Deutro Isaiah energy in combination with that of the Nazarene.

Chung Fu, would you explain to me again what happened with John, Zoroaster, and Yeshua when Yeshua was being baptized?

Yeshua approached the Jordan mainly to stop John from preaching. He was sent by the Essene community to reprimand John for preaching the Essene's secrets. Although Yeshua knew that it would not be necessary to reprimand because John knew who Yeshua was. The very fact that Yeshua came to him, made John realize that his teaching was over, he was silenced and from that point on he might as well stop. John pushed Yeshua under the water as a symbol of release of the old, of getting rid of all the preconceived ideas and to look at the Torah, at Judaism, in a new light. The symbol of this freedom, of the release of all of those things of the past (the subconscious mind) was the dove.

When Yeshua rose from the water he no longer had any of those parts of his previous life there to interfere with his communication. He did not have all power, for if you do not have your subconscious mind and your ego you are not all powerful. Without your subconscious mind and ego you do not judge, or have fear, or frustration, or anger. You are able to perceive and to work and deal with people positively without having to go through the replaying of all the things that you've learned. They are naturally a part of you and only the positive is projected. When Yeshua walked away he began his teaching. John was arrested the next day.

Chung Fu, do you think that the world is better off by Yeshua having come even though his teachings and his life have been misrepresented?

Yes. The world has a better energy. It has an energy that he gave that no one believed; "Love your enemies." The teaching that we bring forth—"Love is the complete acceptance of the other being unconditionally"—and that what you dislike you forget and see only the beauty that is within them. That one energy, that one factor, was important.

Yeshua was the reincarnation of Zoroaster. What was the contribution of other masters like Pythagoras, Confucius, Buddha, Teotechnican, Lao Tzu?

Each of these was an energy input in his part of the world. Both Lao Tzu and Confucius came because China had more people than most of the rest of the world, even at that time. Pythagoras was a catalyst who set up the Essen colony called the "Therapeuti," not those of Qumran. Each of these masters had existed before, and returned and taught as individuals within their time. Zoroaster was a master only because of the Nazarene. Now this may be a little difficult to understand, but it is part of an energy cycle. Remember that the Zoroastrians were instrumental in developing the Pharisees. The followers of Zoroaster were called Parasees and much of their teaching was adopted by the Pharisetic part of the Judaic faith. The Nazarene got his basic teaching from the Pharisees. Zoroaster was at what you may call the "initiate stage." He was highly evolved. He was a master image because it was through that energy that the Nazarene would return. It was what you may call a "catalytic force" that was first united in the Parasees, followed through Babylon into Judea, and eventually within the Pharisetic tradition that the Nazarene was taught. The Pharisaic tradition died not too long after and a whole new change took. There are still Pharisees, but not in the strong tradition.

You might call Zoroaster and Yeshua the same energy for they are. They were an energy that ignited, or began to establish the power and force during the period of the Roman Empire. The Roman Empire was chosen because communication was spread to England, all through Europe, throughout the known African world, even into Hindu, areas of Turkey, and what was Yugoslavia. It was one of those periods of energy that was unbelievable. Babylon did not have that level of communication. The other masters had completed their cycles as initiates and had returned to deal specifically and soundly with maintaining an energy during the 500-year period before Yeshua. It was not only the great prophet of Deutro Isaiah, but also Socrates and Plato, and the Etruscan civilization. It was an energy force and it set the fuse in Babylon.

Chung Fu, could we know the names of the seven disciples please?

Judas, James the Just, John, Peter, Bartholomew, Simon Peter, and lastly Barnabas. The first four were the ones we have talked about the most. Bartholomew was the brother of John, and they were closely connected. Bartholomew stayed with the Christian Church in Jerusalem and did not move from there.

Chung Fu, did these original twelve tribes that you talked about earlier develop their own religion?

Negative. They had many little gods; they had gods of wheat, gods of family, gods of virginity but their main god or source was Abraham. Abraham was the patriarch of the twelve tribes and the only time that they would come together was to talk of Abraham.

Chung fu, how different was their calendar during that time compared to ours?

Drastically different. Time was measured not necessarily in what our current calendar calls months. During the Roman period, the one that was created by Caesar, had 13 months and the Justinian one had 12 months. The Aramaic calendar that was created by Alexander the Great contained 10 months. The one the Jews used (or Judea or David or Solomon) was based on the cycles of the moon as it came and went. It started at high noon at the Winter Solstice and was measured to the low moon, and so it fluctuated between 11 and 13 months. It was regulated in regards to moons rather than to days or dates. The days and dates were only applied much later.

The Judaic history shows that they got their calendar from Babylon and tied it to the time of Moses. It only became adjusted to its present form in approximately 300 CE. The Mayans had a more accurate calendar in 1500 BCE than the one used in Judea. The Egyptians had a calendar with an $11\frac{1}{2}$ to $12\frac{1}{2}$ months cycle, which was also more accurate.

Chung Fu, what was the purpose of making Judas a traitor, betraying Yeshua for pieces of gold, by the Christian writers?

Why else would he hang himself? Why else would the money that they had disappear? If you were one of the disciples, one of the people on the outside, and all of a sudden someone around you hanged himself and the money disappeared, what would you have thought? It was a natural deduction but only James, John and Peter knew the truth and they could not tell.

Chung Fu, you said that the masters that you have spoken about were on their last cycle here. Where are they now, what role do they play and what role will they play in the future?

The question is not where they are. Let us say, for want of an analogy, that Old Chinese was one of them and that as part of his evolution in the dimension that he is in now, he has to spend time communicating with your plane to keep a vibration at a certain level. But at the same time, the energy where he is, is combined with many others and he is communicating with many other dimensions and working with many other aspects.

Old Chinese is not only communicating through vehicle upon your earth plane, but he is communicating with other vehicles and other earth planes in your physical dimension. This is part of his evolution in the dimension that he is in, but it is not a physical place. He can only communicate with you through his last existence because you are a visual people. He is not an Old Chinese in all of the other areas. In some of them he is a Bangwok, or he can be a tree, or he can be a color. The important point is that the masters are an energy and they are a more consolidated energy where they are.

An initiate is created when he has finished what he has come to do with his karma and then goes beyond that. He creates more as an initiate and does it in silence. He returns only because of the energy that he is and what he has created by stepping above the earth plane within his existence. A master can only return after he has completed your plane by stepping into another dimension rather than going back to the spiritual world.

Didn't Yeshua receive some of his early training in the far east?

Negative

Has the second Messiah appeared or will he appear?

Negative

What is the meaning of the bread and the wine? Does it stand for the sacrificial lamb or does it stand for our own body and blood?

Sacrificial lamb. It was the symbol that the Essenes adopted because they did not want to have to do the slaughtering that was done in the temple. It was a symbol of the blood and the body of the lamb. The blood-letting was the symbol of Abraham. Abraham was willing to sacrifice Isaac upon the altar and the very fact that at the end he did not have to became the symbol of the freeing of the nation and the individual. From that point on Abraham was given a lamb to sacrifice as a symbol in the place of Isaac.

Chung Fu, recently it has been said that there are some sayings of Yeshua that were discovered in Egypt that were supposedly written by Ditimus Thomas. Is this true and are these his sayings?

Yes. It is true and they are true.

Chung Fu, could you tell us something about the expression "Christ Light?"

The "Christ Light" is the energy that an individual perceives in understanding. It would be the new understanding of a scripture or a phrase or a person. It would be being able to teach or see something old and familiar for the first time in a new way to excite you. How many of you have stumbled, walked over, and been a part of something for years, and all of a sudden it hits you in the posterior and you realize, "That is what it has been all the time." In a roundabout way that's the Christ Light. It is an energy that you deal with in perceiving. It is a unique energy but it is an interpretive one; a very powerful one.

Were Yeshua and the Nazarene one and the same?

Old Chinese uses Yeshua pre-baptism, Nazarene after the baptism.

Old Chinese, how many books of the New Testament are now being directly attributed to the seven apostles or disciples?

Not one. Paul wrote thirteen, but he was not one of the disciples. Those attributed to Peter were done by Paul. This is not a new discovery. It has been the belief by many in your world. They will discover others by Paul, as he left letters every place. He was one of the most prolific writers of the time and one of the most powerful contributors to Christianity.

You are a part of a physical plane. Within this physical plane you must experience certain things: positive, negative, sexual attitudes, emotion, mental, and elation in all the senses. It does not matter how you experience them, but you must experience them. At times individuals come into this world that have a perception, or creativity, or a oneness within the place that they are in and they can create a more perceptual energy for that time. When they do, they should experience it, feel it, find the light within it. The Nazarene that you perceived or saw was a man. He created an energy just by his being, not something that he wanted to create, for if his desire had been to create it, it would not have been created. That is the Tao.

This is what you should understand; that the people had grabbed on to that mystery, to those teachings. Christianity allowed individuals to be able to step out of one major thing—the temple—and into a church. The female became a part of it. Christianity enabled the average working man to be a part of the teaching. It permitted a disbursement of energy. It allowed people to create and to fight and to have wars. There needs to be poverty and so people can be concerned about that.

Christianity had to be created so that the energy of the earth plane could continue. If this had not occurred something else would have had to have been created to allow wars to be fought. If you want war to be fought you create a thought of which there is a "fuzzy" beginning and let people fight about it. Christianity was important to help maintain the experiences that you must learn upon this plane.

Learn to step above poverty, war, disease, and famine. Christianity has created all of them in every part of the world. And it will be through Christianity and its energy that the individuals who have come from the Judaic-Christian way will be instrumental in allowing the energy of the transference of the next cataclysm, because they have come through one of the most concentrated, most powerful energy centers that this earth has had. They have experienced their indoctrination through hearing "This is what you have to believe." Being able to release oneself from guilt and difficulties is valuable and will be valuable in the future. Christianity allows one to evolve and continue one's growth.

The religions of Buddhism, Shintoism, Taoism, Confucianism, and Islam in one way or another have all created war, poverty, and famine and that is why they exist. Each of the founding individuals came to give a spark, a teaching and if you go back to the center you find what it is all about. But a part of reaching that center is wading through everything that has been created. The center of the Nazarene was, "Love your neighbor and love your enemy." This is the key and "it is within that you will find the kingdom."

Many of your Christian friends are struggling. This is where most of you have been before. You are now perceiving yourself as the core and seeing that you are that light. What is it all about? It is all about learning that you are God, that you are Yahweh. When you have the fortitude, the inner strength, enough guts to say "Yahweh" because you believe that is what you are, your cycle is finished.

POSTSCRIPT

To those who have just read the story of Yeshua one might be disappointed or even consider it sacrilegious that all those reported miracles such as the sermon on the mount, his crucifixion, or even his being the "One Son of God" are not necessarily true. But it is really GOOD NEWS! What IS true is that Yeshua spoke of LOVE as the center of our existence. God is LOVE and we were created in his image: We are LOVE. We, too, are part of the One Son of God just like Yeshua, and He is like our older brother pointing the way for us to go. Everyone and everything in the universe are also part of the One Son of God. Although people's behavior can seem otherwise, each of us has within us the same Divine spark. All of us are on our journey back to God; a journey without distance.

"Christ" literally means "the anointed one." And we are all the "Christ;" the anointed Son of God, who created us. This unifies us with each other and with God. Therefore, the apparent separation that we all feel, not only from God, but also from each other, is an illusion. Yeshua was indeed an awakened individual who came to the earth plane to speak of brotherly LOVE. With his extensive training in healing and perception, plus being without any ego, his charisma must have been awesome. Just being near him would have awakened many.

Modern Christianity got it wrong when they insisted that Yeshua was the "only" Son of God. How did this happen? How did Yeshua's simple message of "LOVE your neighbor and your enemy" get co-opted by religion into something quite different? For almost two thousand years Christianity has been used as justification to kill our brothers as in the crusades and the Inquisition. Just as the preceding story of Yeshua states, four elements to create a new religion were present at the time of Yeshua:

1. A charismatic leader teaching something old and that thousands believe in, but teaching in a new and different way.
2. A good publicity expert like Paul.
3. The inclusion of women.
4. A leader who is relatively unknown so that his past and accomplishments can be embellished or reconstructed.

Yeshua was a Jew who taught the Torah and the Jewish Scriptures, which were believed by thousands, but he taught them in a new and different way. Paul was amazing, circling the Mediterranean four times, preaching what he thought Yeshua said and who he thought Yeshua was. Paul was a prolific writer and Bible scholars attribute as many as 13 gospels to the writings of Paul. Women were included from the beginning, which was new to the cultures and religions that existed at the time of Yeshua. And Yeshua was relatively unknown so that his teachings and accomplishments could be embellished and in many cases changed altogether.

Yeshua was born in mid-October, but the writers of the New Testament claimed he was born on December 25. Why was this? Pre-existing pagan religions often had a "god" with the same attributes that were eventually bestowed on Yeshua: Born on the 25th of December, born of a virgin, star in the East, known as the "Lamb of God" or the "Light," betrayed and crucified, dead for three days, and resurrected. Here are a few examples of the backgrounds of previous deities:

Horus – Egypt 3000 BCE
- Sun God
- Born on December 25
- Born of the virgin Isis
- Star in the East
- Adored by three kings
- At age 12 a prodigal teacher
- At age 30 baptized and started his ministry
- Had 12 disciples, performed miracles
- Known as "the Lamb of God," "Good Sheppard," "the Light"
- Betrayed and crucified
- Dead for three days and then resurrected

Attis – Greece 1200 BCE
- Born on December 25
- Born of a virgin
- Crucified
- Dead for three days and then resurrected

Mithras – Persia 1200 BCE
- Born on December 25
- Born of a virgin
- 12 disciples
- Performed miracles
- Known as "the Truth," "the Lamb of God"
- Dead for three days and then resurrected
- Established Sunday as day of worship

Krishna – India 900 BCE
- Born of a virgin
- Star in the East
- Performed miracles
- Resurrected

Dionysus – Greece 500 BCE
- Born December 25
- Born of a virgin
- Performed miracles including water into wine
- Traveled and taught
- Known as "King of Kings," "God's only begotten Son," "the Alpha and Omega"

Now consider the aspects attributed to Yeshua:
- Born on December 25
- Born of a virgin
- Star in the East
- Three kings
- Prodigy teacher at age 12
- Baptized at age 30 and began his ministry
- Performed miracles
- Known as "the King of Kings," "the only Son of God"
- Betrayed and crucified
- Dead for three days and then resurrected.

The writers of the New Testament borrowed from previous cultures, knowing that these attributes would help establish Yeshua as a God and a leader of a new religion. While Yeshua's message was, in essence, more powerful than all that was made up, these assigned attributes were necessary to create a powerful religion that could corral people.

How could all these pagan gods be born on the 25th of December when in many cases the calendar was totally different from the one we use today? No matter what the calendar was in use at the time, the three days after the Winter Solstice was a time of rebirth of the sun. The sun was often worshiped as the symbol of God in that it gave light and life to all on the earth. On the Winter Solstice, usually the 21st or 22nd of December in our calendar, the sun appears at the lowest point in the south making the daytime (light) the shortest of the year and the nighttime (darkness) the longest. The Sun then seems to stall there for three days before it begins its ascent to the north, giving more and more light each day to the earth. It is easy to see why cultures chose this auspicious time to mark their god's birthday. Yeshua was also given this time as his birthday to imbue him with the same importance as was given to the previous pagan gods. In actuality, Yeshua was born in mid-October of our calendar.

Being born of a virgin gives the gods the mantle of purity. This is necessary to set the individual apart from the rest of humanity so that he can be worshiped as special. Being "special" increases our feelings of separation from God and from each other.

The star in the east is Sirius. And the three kings are the three stars of Orion's belt that are the brightest at this time and point directly to the star, Sirius. At the Winter Solstice, these stars are very bright and point to the sunrise on the 25th; the birth of the sun. This propitious time can be used to signify an important event, like the birth of a god.

The Bible reports that Yeshua began his ministry after he was baptized at the age of 30 as with many of the previous gods. In actuality, he was 40, but the writers of the New Testament needed to align with the previous signs that were known by the populace of the time.

Having 12 disciples or followers or brothers was also common with the previous gods. And so, too, was it written that Yeshua had 12 disciples. Twelve is a common number throughout the Bible and history: the 12 tribes of Israel, the 12 constellations of the Zodiac. Having 12 disciples made it jive with the previous gods. According to our story, Yeshua had seven disciples, not 12.

On the Winter Solstice the sun appears "dead" for three days before it begins its ascent northward. Thus, three days have been used many times between the death of a god and his resurrection. Betrayal and crucifixion are also common attributes of previous gods. It was easy for the New Testament writers to adopt this form of death, as that is what appeared to have happened. No one was at the crucifixion of Yeshua's substitute, except perhaps Peter, who, it was reported, denied three times that the person being crucified was indeed Yeshua.

Thomas Paine (1737–1809) stated the following:
- "The Christian religion is a parody on the worship of the sun, in which they put a man called Christ in the place of the sun, and pay him the adoration originally paid to the sun."

The ancient Egyptian religion seemed to serve as a basis for the Judaic/Christian religion that followed. The Egyptian religion included baptism, an afterlife, a final judgment, crucifixion, Passover, virgin birth, death & resurrection, saviors, communion, Easter and Christmas.

Due to the lack of Yeshua being mentioned by the early history writers of the time, many feel that Yeshua was a made-up figure. A handful of historians, including Josephus (37–100 CE), did mention Yeshua, but only briefly. This is not surprising, considering Yeshua's short ministry and the lack of media at the time of his life. The fact that He was mentioned at all is quite amazing and seems to be proof that he did exist.

The persecution of the early Christians by the Roman Empire began around 64 CE and continued for the next two and a half centuries. In 311 CE the Roman Emperor Constantine (272–337 CE) de-criminalized Christianity as a religion and in 325 CE Constantine called the First Council of Nicaea where church dogma began to put structure and form over the simpler, but extraordinary messages of Yeshua: "Love *One Another*" and the "*Kingdom of Heaven is Within.*"

— PART 2 —
YESHUA TODAY

INTRODUCTION

After Yeshua was NOT crucified and he traveled to the mountains of Jordan with his three disciples (James, Peter, and John), he taught them wisdoms that were beyond what he normally taught the populace of Judea. What might have he said to just the three? What would Yeshua say to us today? How can we know?

Fortunately, Yeshua has come back to us in modern times through the channeling by Helen Schucman with the support of Bill Tethford, both of whom are now deceased. From 1965 until 1972 Helen received "voices" that she identified as coming from Yeshua and which she wrote down each evening. In the morning she took her notes to her co-worker, Bill Tethford, to type up, creating the original manuscript. Both Schucman and Tethford were PhDs in clinical psychology working for the Columbia Presbyterian Medical Center in New York City.

After completion of the original manuscript, a fellow PhD and psychologist, Kenneth Wapnick, appeared on the scene and at their invitation reviewed the transcribed material. Upon reading the manuscript, Wapnick abandoned his previous plans to become a monk at a Trappist Monastery in Israel and began organizing the material into chapters and subheadings, also numbering each sentence for reference. The results were published in a book entitled "A Course in Miracles" (ACIM) which serves as the inspiration for Part Two of this book. When quoting Yeshua his sayings will be in italics and underlined and when quoting "A Course in Miracles" they will be in italics. LOVE capitalized refers to Divine LOVE while love in lower case refers to human love.

Wapnick went on to teach the material full-time and founded, with his wife Gloria, the Foundation for A Course in Miracles (FACIM), in Temecula, California. After Wapnick's passing, the Foundation re-located to Henderson, Nevada

While skeptics may question the authorship of the ACIM material as being from Yeshua, I have no doubt that what is written is connected with the energy that was Yeshua. The ideas put forth in ACIM are consistent with the story told by Chung Fu about the Nazarene and his teachings. In the following chapters, I have taken liberally from the ACIM text many ideas that Yeshua most likely would have taught his three closest disciples. Ideas that at the time of Yeshua would have seemed totally unknown and that even today may seem contrary to the way most people see the world.

A modern Yeshua tells us "the way" with his channeling through Helen Schucman. As was the case 2,000 years ago, people may not see the truth and wisdom of his words. And even if they do most will not live them. It is only up to us to follow his Light to Awakening and Enlightenment.

Once again, two thousand years later, Yeshua is asking us to believe in LOVE as the organizing force of the Universe and our only True Reality.

— CHAPTER SIX —
OUR ORIGIN

We are, and still remain, an idea in the Mind of God. We were created by God as the Son of God and are One with the Creator. We, as the One, exist in Heaven within God and experience only the LOVE of God. There are no conflicts, nothing outside of our union with God. We are exactly the same as God with the only difference being that He created us, we did not create Him (although much of the Old Testament has God in the image of man, not man in the image of God.) It has been said that God created us and then we returned the favor.

Being the same as God, we can co-create with Him by extending LOVE; that is our only function in Heaven. And we are still in Heaven right now, at One with God. That is our ONLY true reality.

In this blissful state of total LOVE, Peace, and Joy came a *"tiny mad idea"* of what it would be like to be special and separate from God. This mad idea of being separate from God was a result of wanting some sort of recognition from Him, to be special and individual. As soon as this idea occurred to us, the One Son of God, it was corrected by God and nothing in Heaven was changed. God and Heaven are changeless so that "...*not one note in Heaven's song was missed.*"

However, the One Son of God *"forgot to laugh"* at this tiny mad idea and believed that separation from God was possible and so began our DREAM of the illusion of separation. The first separated thought was our decision as the One Son of God to abandon God and make our own kingdom. The problem never was the *"tiny mad idea"* of separation from God, but our incorrect belief that it was possible.

As Rumi, the 13th century Persian poet, said:

"This is a dream, only a sleeper considers it real."

"A man goes to sleep in the town where he has always lived, and he dreams he is living in another town, In the dream he doesn't remember the town he is sleeping in, in his bed. The world is that kind of sleep."

In our DREAM of separation from God, the Son of God's one Mind became split and we became an observer/decision-maker choosing between the two parts of our split Mind. *"We are either the observer in the dream or the figure in the dream."* One part of our Mind made the EGO consciousness, which has us being a perceiver rather than a creator. The Ego's thought system is one of separation from God. The other part of our Mind is the remembrance that we are One with God and there is no separation. At every moment the observer/decision-maker is choosing either the ego (fear and judgement) or God (LOVE and Forgiveness) in response to any person or event. Remembering our eternal Oneness with God as our only reality is the real Atonement. The Mind and the split-mind should not be confused with our brains, which came later along with our bodies.

The separation never occurred but the belief that separation was possible and indeed had happened caused the Son (Us) a great amount of SIN, GUILT, and FEAR; SIN that we left the Love of God (we didn't actually), GUILT from our belief that we abandoned God, and FEAR of revenge and reprisal by God if we were ever found out. Many Christian Churches have made sin a mortal offense. (The word "sin" actually comes from an archery term meaning "missing the mark" and is therefore correctable.) The Christian Church's idea of "original sin" is our thinking that we have left God (as in the Adam and Eve story) and we are condemned. But this just isn't true, as we have never left the side of God. It is only in our dream that we believe we left God.

Immersed in sin, guilt, and fear we became totally distraught. The ego, which we made, came to the Son's apparent rescue by suggesting we make a universe (the "big bang") where the Son could hide and so be safe. And to make finding us even more difficult, the One Son of God fragmented into trillions times trillions of separate entities, which included our bodies, making up the universe and reflecting the initial separation from God. This is all a DREAM and an ILLUSION since in reality the One Son of God is still in Heaven with God and is merely dreaming of separation.

Time and space were seemingly created in our illusion when the universe was created. There is no time or space in Heaven, which is our only true reality. But in our dream our belief in Sin (past), Guilt (present), and Fear (future) combined to create TIME and our belief in separation created SPACE. When sin, guilt, and fear are projected out it created linear time. These are ego constructs and exist only in the dream. There is no time or space in the Mind of God or His One Son. Without sin, guilt, and fear, there is no time; it collapses. Without the belief in separation there is no space. Since the ego inhabits the body, we need to shift our focus from the body to our Minds (not our brains.) We erroneously believe that our minds are in our body but in actuality our bodies are in our Mind. All our problems and pain are caused by our underlying guilt of thinking we have left God, which in most cases is deeply unconscious.

By identifying with the ego, we created a double-shield from our memory of being the One Son of God. First, we believed we actually separated from God and created an ego thought system that encompassed our sin, guilt, and fear. Finding this painful and unacceptable, our ego came up with the plan of creating an actual physical world of separation and fragmentation, including our bodies, where we could hide out from a "wrathful god," a place where God could not enter and we would be safe. Second, a veil of forgetfulness was established between our ego thought system and the physical world making us unaware that we even had a Mind that could decide against the ego and for the Divine. As long as we remain mindless our ego is safe from our choosing the Divine (LOVE and Forgiveness) which would dissipate the ego's thought system (judgement and separation) from our split minds.

Consciousness was the first split introduced into the Mind after our seeming separation. This created a subject and object point of reference and resulted in the dualistic nature of the earth plane. In true reality there is no personal self. On the earth plane the personal self is busily engaged in getting, achieving, accomplishing, accumulating, whereas our real Self is giving, bestowing, sharing, and blessing. When we believed in the separation, we left our larger Self for our little self. Through this apparent separation we lost our connection to God's LOVE which left us in a state of lack. From the moment a baby is born it experiences an overwhelming feeling of lack and is dependent on outside forces as it needs to breathe and eat to stay alive. Our lives then continue requiring outside support and gratification.

"Who am I" and _"Why am I here"_ have been the perennial questions philosophers and theologians have grappled with over the centuries. To find out who we really are has been humanity's goal. Who we are is Spirit and we are having a physical experience in a body, or at least dreaming that we are. We created this dream world (the earth plane) in order to feel separate and individual. As we Awaken from the dream, we become Aware of who we truly are and begin to express, more and more, our innate nature, which is LOVE. The reason we are here is to extend that LOVE and so become the Light of the world.

This illusion of the dream world cost India the efforts of thousands of years to unmask. This same illusion the West has labored, just as hard, to maintain and strengthen. Nothing really changes in our dream world; sickness, greed, war, pain, and with bodies that are made to break and go wrong and to be alone, suffer, then die. We are confused as to what the cause is of our suffering and we constantly attribute our problems to things outside ourselves. *The Mind is the actual Cause and the world and our bodies are the Effect.* The world has it backward, thinking that our problems are solvable with our bodies and changing our outward conditions, but the solutions are always in our Minds.

Lao Tzu, the 6th century philosopher, author of the Tao Te Ching, and founder of the Tao Philosophy, is reported as saying:

"There is no need to running outside for better seeing
Nor to peer from a window
Rather abide at the center of your being
For the more you leave it, the less you learn."

God did not create our illusory world, WE did, or specifically our ego thought system did. All the pain, suffering, wars, disease, and injustices that we see here are from our ego thought system of separation. God only knows us as his One Son who never left His side in Heaven. We are Spirit dreaming of a physical experience in our imagined bodies. *"I am not a body. I am still as God created me."* We will all awaken from this dream and find ourselves still in Heaven, just as we awaken from our nightly dreams (which seem real enough in the dream) and find ourselves still in bed. To awaken we only need to discipline our thoughts and actions away from the ego thoughts of being separate from God and others and to encompass love and forgiveness in every situation.

This simple nursery rhyme says it all:

Row, row, row, your boat (us)
Gently down the stream (life)
Merrily, merrily, merrily, merrily (be happy)
Life is but a dream (an illusion)

— CHAPTER SEVEN —

THE UNIVERSE

Our theory suggests that the physical universe came into being by a thought from the One Son of God. The One Son had a silly idea, a whim, of what it would be like to be separate from God. Instead of laughing at this preposterous idea and dismissing it immediately, the One Son believed it was possible and the ego was born, as a thought of separation from God. Actually, leaving our Creator, who gave us existence, was not even possible but the One Son entered a dream where separation was not only possible but seemed to have actually happened.

The idea of leaving God was very disturbing to the One Son. How could we leave God, our Creator? Leaving God would be like we were killing Him and His Love for us. But thinking we were trapped in the now dream of separation we did feel like we had abandoned our Creator. Our guilt for thinking we killed God was so powerful and all-pervasive that we longed for a solution to rid us of our guilt, and most likely the wrath of God who would surely hunt us down and punish us severely (think of the Old Testament's wrathful God). The ego thought system of separation came to the One Son of God's rescue (or damnation) by creating a universe where God would not be present and we could hide out. With this one thought the universe was created in a flash; a big bang.

The One Son of God split into trillions upon trillions of separate parts creating all the stars, planets, and everything in the universe including you and me, all the plants and animals, all the earth and stones…everything. In addition, time and space were also created, which did not exist before, when we had existed as one with God. The thought of separation, not only from God, but from each other, created space. The linear expansion of the universe with sin, guilt, and fear, created time; past, present, and future (which also did not exist prior to the universe).

While our dream of separation seems real, it is just a dream; an illusion. In Reality we are still the One Son of God dreaming of this alternate reality. God is LOVE, and created his One Son in his own image as LOVE. This is who we really are: LOVE. We are just like God with the only difference being that he created us; we did not create him. We are really still with God as his One Son and have not separated or left Him. In a way, God does not know about our dream. To Him we are just sleeping.

In less than a nanosecond the entire universe rolled out like a carpet containing every possible life, condition, event, and circumstance and then rolled right back up again. This happened so quickly that it was not even noticed. Yet, the One Son of God continued in his dream of this no longer existing reality. We continue in our dream of this often nightmarish saga even though it has never really existed. It seems very real to us here just as our nighttime dreams seem real until we awake from our sleep and find ourselves still in our beds. It is up to us to Awaken from this dream of separation and know that we are LOVE and not separate from God, or each other, or everything in the universe. When we truly Awaken from this dream of separation, the entire universe will disappear from our consciousness, for it never ever really existed in the first place.

The early Gnostics attempted to solve the riddle of why a loving, forgiving, and accepting God would create a world full of pain, suffering, wars, poverty, greed, etc. by believing that the universe was created by a "lesser" God. They believed that God is incorruptible and could not have within Him such a place. The idea of the One Son of God having a "whim" of separation may also be a metaphor to accomplish the same result; an explanation why such a world exists.

It seems paradoxical that while the One Son of God created the universe to escape from God, God stayed with us. God is in us and in everything in the universe: the plants, animals, birds, stones, air, molecules, atoms…everything. The God energy is abundant and unlimited and is our birthright; we just block it. The yogis refer to this energy as Shakti, the Chinese as Chi, and the West as Spirit. This energy is available to us and can be harnessed to accomplish any creation that we want. Sages throughout the ages have known this and it has recently been brought forth through the book and movie *The Secret* and through proponents of "The Law of Attraction."

— CHAPTER EIGHT —
TIME AND SPACE

Time and space do not exist in heaven or in dimensions beyond the earth plane. How did we get time and space in our universe? When the One Son of God had the silly idea of what it would be like to be separate from God, and did not laugh at this impossibility, we believed it was possible to be separate and so began our dream; the illusion of being separate. In Reality we have never left God, but we are dreaming of being separate. Our separate bodies prove to us that we are separate from each other and from God. This idea of separation actually created space; that there must be space between us if I am here and you are over there. In the eternity of the One there is no space.

Our resultant belief in the separation also made us guilty that we actually left God which is mostly buried in our subconscious. The fear that God will find us and punish us for separating created the future. Guilt and fear created the idea of us having a past and a future and thus time in a linear fashion. If we don't have any guilt or fear (which is true) then we have no need for time and can reside only in the present.

Spiritual teachers tell us the way to enlightenment is to be constantly in the present, not the past or future. Ram Dass wrote

Be Here Now in the early 70s and Eckhart Tolle wrote *The Power of Now* in the early 2000s. Both teachings point the way to awakening is to live in the present moment, the now. Yet most of us live mainly in the past or the future. We often get our identity from our past and hope that our future will be better than our present. If only this _____ were different then I could be happy, satisfied, and content. We live mostly in the memory of the past or anticipation of the future. The future is imagined as being better (hope) or worse (anxiety) and both are illusions. Accepting the "what is" of the present moment is difficult for most of us, but this is the only reality and is the only point of access to the timeless world of "Being."

"Monkey Mind" is the term often given for our rampant thoughts that flow in our minds like a wild river, seemingly uncontrollable by us. We live in these thoughts which tie us to the past and from which we obtain our identity and most often give us anxiety and unease when we think of our future. Identifying with these thoughts is food for our egos. It keeps us tied to the non-existent past and fear for the future. Our egos were constructed by us to validate our feelings of separation. Its middle name is "more" and is never satisfied. Our egos try and keep us from the present now as its existence is only in the past or future. Staying in the present is death to our egos. Everything happens in the now.

So much of the world's population is tortured by our minds. Guilt and fear reign supreme in the constant thoughts running through our brains. We try to escape the pain, the anxiety, the fears, etc. with our addictions to alcohol, drugs, food, shopping, judgements, complaining, sickness, etc. Chung Fu once stated "thought forms are nails in the coffin of our spiritual development." Being present means no thoughts of past or future exist and we are free to experience our natural state of divine beings.

We of course need to pay attention to ordinary time. We make appointments, the bus comes on schedule, we show up for work "on time." Tolle refers to this as "clock time" and we need to stay alert to clock time to function in our world. But living in the past time or future time is a barrier to our awakening to who we really are: the One Son of God LOVED and cherished by God.

By moving from the false sense of ourselves, created by identifying with our past, we are able to reside more often in the present moment. Yeshua stated *"before Abraham was, I am."* He did not say "before Abraham, I was," which would have implied the existence of time. By identifying only with the present being of his inner Divinity Yeshua became the "Christ." We too have this ability; being with our Divine essence in the present and releasing our identification with the past and future. Yeshua brought the dimension of eternity into our world. God said "I am that I am." Nothing more.

— CHAPTER NINE —
REALITY

Our true reality is being One with God, and in this Reality we are so absorbed in God that we are God. The only difference between us and God in this true Reality is that God created us; we did not create God. Other than this, we and God are one. There is no second or third, only the One of which we are. Like a hologram, each individual part is the complete whole as well. We are like a drop out of the ocean that feels its own separateness but contains the whole ocean within its separateness. And when the drop returns to the ocean, it **IS** the ocean once again.

Our thoughts create our world view and our sense of self and reality. Our perceptions are a reflection of the state of our Mind. The world is a creation of our Minds. Buddha proclaimed, "We are what we think. All that we are arises with our thoughts. With our thoughts we make the world." Yet we often seek to know the world without first knowing ourselves and the power of our thoughts.

Another word for God could be LOVE, for that is God's essence. It is also true that we were created in God's image and, being created by LOVE, that is our essence too. We are LOVE. Our purpose is to extend this Divine LOVE and thus become a creator just like God. This is a never ending process and goes on for infinity. Well, actually even longer, because in this reality there is no time or space, so even the concept of infinity does not exist.

In this Reality there are no "bodies," just energy or spirit. If this is so, where are we now? In fact, we are still with God and just dreaming of being body here on the earth plane. This is hard for us to understand, I know. I once met a man who was so convinced that the earth plane is a substantial reality that when I told him we existed in a dream he wanted to smack me on the side of my head to prove this life is real. Even though my body would feel the smack while in the dream, it is still a dream.

Everything exists within God but God cannot be defined. The Tao stated that the God that can be named is not God. First, we need to know who we really are. The Secret Gospels said, "Whoever does not know Self does not know anything. But whoever does know Self, already has acquired knowledge about the depth of the Universe." Being consumed by the material world blocks our awakening to reality. If we do not fast from the world we will not be able to find the kingdom within, which is our true reality.

When the Buddha was asked by his followers whether he was a saint or a god, he replied that he was just Awake; Awake from the dream of being separate from God. Masters of the past and those yet to come know this world is an illusion and are awake from the dream and know their true Reality. Many spiritual seekers state that they just want to "Awaken," which in actuality is just what is needed.

This world seems real to us. But think of our nighttime dreams where, no matter how preposterous events may be, we believe they are real while in the dream. I remember one dream where I was chasing a man and when he approached a lake he turned into a duck and swam away. In the dream I did not question this absurdity.

We have both physical and emotional experiences in our dreams that seem real enough. But when we awaken, we find ourselves still in our bed and all those dreams go "poof" and vanish, as if they never happened. It is the same in the earth plane dream and when we Awake from this dream we'll find that we are still with God and have always been so. And this earth dream will go "poof" as well.

When we look at the world and don't like what we see we most likely want to change it. But the world is just a reflection of our inner state; like looking into a mirror. If we don't like the image in the mirror it won't change anything by attacking the mirror. It may even hurt us by doing so and would be a form of insanity if we tried. If we accept the image as "what is" and even make friends with the image we retain our inner peace. This is the only true way to transform the world.

If this life here on earth is an illusion—just a dream—why should we pay any attention to it? To deny that our actions and our body are not real is an unworthy form of denial. While our focus is here in this separated state a wonderful opportunity exists to re-connect with the LOVE of God which is ever present, even in the dream. It may seem a paradox that we need to be in the dream as if it were real and also know that it is not the true Reality. The opportunity is for us to step beyond this material world into a life of Spirit without leaving the world; to be in the world but not of it. It is here that we can make progress in our consciousness of who we really are; even more so than in the spirit world. And all progress is through re-connecting to the LOVE that we are and expressing this LOVE.

To re-connect to the LOVE that we are we want to be kind to everyone and everything. We need to practice mindfulness by always remembering who we really are: the loved Son of God. It is a sign of wisdom to know where we came from and who we really are.

— CHAPTER TEN —
LOVE

In many other languages there are several words to reflect the various shades and aspects of love. In English we have but one word to describe the different layers of love; such as God's LOVE, love for family, love for our children, love of our spouse, love for our lover, love for our friends, love for our country, love of knowledge, etc.

To simplify this discussion, we can consider that there are basically two types of love. The one we are most familiar with is "human love." This is often experienced as love between two individuals, usually male and female, although not always the case. Expressions of love in human love are conditional: "As long as you meet my needs, I will continue to love you."

"Falling in love" is a wonderful experience but it is based on a shaky foundation. And it usually only lasts for a short time and is often referred to as the "honeymoon period." This is when our love partner can do no wrong. What seems endearing at first, such as the way they chew their food, becomes an annoying characteristic later on. For example, there was a man who had "fallen in love" with a wonderful woman. Early in their relationship they took a back-country road that was unpaved with almost no traffic. Her car had a flat tire, and upon examining the spare, he saw that it was also flat. She had never had the spare repaired. At the time he thought the whole situation was so funny that he broke into laughter. He thought her failure to fix the spare as cute, even though they were now stranded in a remote location. After a few years into their relationship would he still have found the situation humorous, or would he now consider his wife careless and irresponsible?

There was a cartoon from the 70s depicting a man and woman staring into each other's eyes across a small table obviously in love. The thought bubble above the woman said "my hero" and the thought bubble above the man said "great tits." The caption under the cartoon said "The basis for a perfect love relationship." Funny? Yes, but unfortunately this is often the case.

We may choose partners to fill in the hole we feel about our own persona, even though this is often unconscious. Individuals who feel that they are not good enough or unlovable can find a partner who loves them, and then this hole is filled, at least temporarily. "You complete me" is often stated as a reason for our love for another.

So often this human love fades and the love evaporates, and many times turns to hate because our great expectations were not fulfilled. Partners can feel betrayed when their loved one fails to deliver the "promised" fulfilling of their needs. I have often heard people say "the person I seek to love must be able to fulfill my needs." This foundation for human love is shaky because it assumes that we and others are not whole and complete just as we are and we need someone outside ourselves to make us whole and happy. Our happiness now depends on someone else. This incompleteness may be true for our persona and for our bodies, but is not true for who we really are: the Loved Son of God.

Chung Fu put forth the idea that, generally speaking, men have an outward positive projection and an inner negative point. This is not bad or good, it is more like electricity which has both a positive and a negative charge in order to be balanced. Like an electrical plug, which is either negative (socket) or positive (prongs,) the human form is similar in energy. Man, with an internal negative polarity, is usually attracted to a woman who has an internal positive polarity and an outward negative polarity. In both the internal and outward polarity there is a balance within a male-female relationship, as positive and negative polarities are in balance. There is usually a natural attraction to the opposite sex in order to achieve a balance of these negative and positive polarities. While our soul or higher self is complete and whole, the human bodies into which we incarnate are physically only one half of the whole, which makes us attractive to the opposite sex in order to achieve some sort of wholeness.

Another type of love is "true love." True love is like Divine LOVE in that it is unconditional. The LOVE from God is not conditional upon one's behavior. No matter what, God LOVES us. We can make mistakes, do wrong, even sin, and God still LOVES us. He is our father and forgives us for all our seeming transgressions. God is like the father in the parable of "the Returning Son." Even though the son has squandered all his inheritance on women, song, and rich foods, his father rejoices his return and his love for his son is not diminished. It even seems that the father's love is increased as his son's journey has made the son's awareness deeper and more profound.

True love in human form is a shadow of this Divine LOVE of God but has the same unconditional nature as Divine LOVE. God's LOVE cannot really be described only experienced. It is a pure experience that is beyond words.

True love can be defined as the unconditional acceptance of another. While this type of love is rare between men and women, it is possible. And while this love does not mandate that you stay together—for example in an abusive relationship—it does require that you see beyond the other's behavior to the inner spirit of the person. The reason true love is rare is that it must be between two individuals who are whole within themselves and are not requiring outside verification of who they are to feel love and to be happy.

The goal is to have true love in all of our relationships, not with just our partner. Expressing true love is so close to Divine LOVE that experiencing it here on the earth plane is a wonderful ambition. Achieving it with a partner can be the most difficult challenge of all because of one's unconscious needs. This is also true with family members. It seems a paradox that to achieve true love it is more difficult with those we think we love (like spouse and family), but this is often the case. A marriage is a great place to practice true love, but it is not for quitters.

To have a successful partnership filled with love between two people, each individual must feel complete within themselves and not require anything outside themselves to feel loved. Working on this type of relationship with a partner and others is a most worthwhile endeavor. God is LOVE and we have been created in His image. In our essence, we are LOVE. Our only true purpose on this earth (and in heaven) is to express and extend LOVE.

The opposite of human love is fear. Human love and fear are the parents of all other emotions. Divine LOVE has no opposite. Whatever form our disquiet take (uneasiness, anger, worry, insecurity, depression and so on), it is unloving and therefore fearful. The fear of not being loved is a basic human problem. Yet we are LOVED by God at all times and forever. It is through our recognition of this LOVE that our salvation and the salvation of the world is assured. In the broadest sense, there is nothing but LOVE. We need to keep reminding ourselves that "LOVE is All There Is." (LIATI)

LOVE is a state of Being. Our LOVE is not outside but deep within us. We can never lose it and it cannot leave us. It is not dependent on some other body or some external form. Yeshua is a thought of LOVE that is non-specific. LOVE is in ALL of us.

Divine LOVE is unlimited in its power and reverses all the laws of the world. It is beyond every restriction of time, space, and limits of any kind. We are holy because all things God has created are holy. Our holiness is totally unlimited in its power because it establishes us as a Son of God, at one with the Mind of our Creator. True LOVE is the salvation of the world because it teaches, not by preaching, but merely by blessing all things. For every five minutes spent in this LOVE 1,000 minds are affected positively.

Humans are always doing only one of two things: expressing love or calling for love. Therefore, our response to any situation or person should always be the same: LOVE. Maintain this thought and we will end all judgment and be of great benefit to ourselves and to others. AND the world will change before our very eyes without having to change anything outside ourselves.

— CHAPTER ELEVEN —
GUILT

The guilt we feel for thinking that we have left God, our Creator, is so overwhelming that most of us have buried it deep within our unconscious. Guilt is a human emotion that is of the lowest negative vibration and we, as humans, want to escape it any way we can. Burying it in our unconscious where it remains out of sight seems like the best solution to escape it. Those negative emotions buried in the unconscious affects us in ways that seem unconnected to our guilt. In an effort to rid ourselves of this buried guilt we tend to project it onto others and thus it seems to be outside ourselves and not part of us. We want to feel innocent, not guilty of leaving God, so we project that guilt onto others in order to get rid of it.

For example, we often blame others for our own problems because it is easier to blame someone or something else for our troubles. By projecting our guilt onto others, it appears that our difficulties are someone else's fault. Just by projecting our guilt onto others, it does not really leave us because *"Ideas leave not their source."* Pushing our guilt onto others keeps it alive within us. The ego exists in a futile attempt to cover over our perceived guilt by projecting it out and onto others or onto events in our lives. The problem with this is that we believe we can escape our underlying guilt by projecting it outward, but this never alleviates our guilt. There is a purpose for our illusory world which is to keep us mindless. Too keep us from knowing that we always have a choice between the ego and the Divine. The world becomes the teaching vehicle for us to understand that we are a Mind, not a body, and we always have a choice between the ego thought system of separation from each other and God and the Divine thought that we are all one.

We mostly think all our problems are outside of us, and the solutions to our issues and world problems are out in the world. The solutions, however, are always in our Minds because all problems are a projection from our Minds. *"Projection proceeds perception."* Trying to solve our problems out in the world is like trying to change the movie by rushing up to the screen where we see the images rather than going to the projector (our Minds) where the real cause is. There is no hierarchy of problems, none that are either greater or smaller, since they all come from the same one source: our buried guilt in thinking we have left God. For solutions to our problems we often demand that God or Yeshua or Mohammed or ___?___ comes down into our dream of the world to solve our made up problems. This is insanity.

How then can we deal with this overwhelming guilt? If left unchecked it can make our lives miserable.

The offer of Atonement was not to relieve us of our sins, but to release all that buried guilt which makes our lives so painful. Atonement is the acceptance of the fact that our separation from God never occurred. There is nothing to feel guilty about. We are still with God, dreaming that we are separate and living here on earth. I know life on the earth plane seems real enough, but so do our nightly dreams when we are dreaming. Awaken to the fact that we are God's Son, we have not killed Him off, and we have not left Him. Bask in the LOVE of God which has never left us. Atonement is the knowledge that we are still with God. Our perceived guilt is baseless.

It is necessary to recognize that guilt is the basis for our projecting negative thoughts onto others. We then focus on the "bad" behavior of others rather than perceiving their divine spark and who they really are. Other people's behavior comes from either their expressing love or calling out for love, nothing else. In either case our response should always be the same: love.

One of the most important things we earthlings can do is to reduce this buried guilt so that we can perceive a more peaceful, caring, and loving world: First, by recognizing that since we did not leave God, there is no basis for this guilt, and Second, to train our minds and therefore our reaction to perceived outside events. Our goal should always be in giving a loving response to every situation that occurs in our lives.

— CHAPTER TWELVE —

FEAR

Love and Fear are the two main emotions that are present on the earth plane. All other emotions come from these two. Anger, sadness, grief, anxiety, worry, dread, tension, greed, judgment, and depression all come from fear. Fear of not being good enough, fear of not being lovable, fear of scarcity and not having enough, and ultimately the suppressed fear that God will take his retribution for us having left Heaven and Him. Fear only exists in the future. Immediate fear or present fear rarely exists today. It is not often that we are chased by a mountain lion or surrounded by sharks while swimming. Those situations could create real fear and not "False Evidence Appearing Real" which is mostly the case.

Fear comes from a concern of the future while Guilt is based on the past; past actions that we wish had not happened. Our egos exist in the past and future, not the present, and they are energized by Fear and Guilt, offering solutions to escape these two emotions through suppression, blaming others, and keeping us out of the present. Neither Fear or Guilt is in the present. The present moment does not exist for the ego. The more we stay in the Now—the present—the less the ego can dominate our thoughts and actions.

The opposite of human love is fear. Divine LOVE has no opposite: LOVE is all there is. Fear is based on something happening in the future, but is not happening in the Now. Our fears come from the ego's fear of annihilation. The ego is constantly defending its illusory identity. Since we dwell in time, the past and the future are what is important to us and our egos, and they occupy our thoughts. The ego does not exist in the present, so being in the present eliminates the ego. We need to remember that we made the ego and can eliminate it as well. The past gives us our identity and the future, a promise of salvation; both are illusions. The only reality is the Now—the present—where our thoughts of the past (Guilt) and of the future (Fear) do not exist. Therefore, the more we identify with the present moment, the more free of pain and suffering we become.

A way to get rid of our problems is to emerge from fear. Suppression is one of the ego tactics that keeps us from directly looking at our fears. Most people deal with fears by working harder, smarter, doing more, accomplishing more, striving more, getting up earlier, being a better person, more generous, more organized, having clearer goals, etc. Trying to change the external situation gives only temporary relief. Allow everything that comes up to be there (accepting the "What Is") and not trying to fix or change anything. We need to invite our internal guidance to come in and switch our thought system from fear to its opposite: love. This takes vigilance every day. This dense world can pull us down to our old habits and reinforce our feelings of separation. We can keep our awareness of our Oneness with God and each other, and our fears will begin to dissipate.

Don't despair when negative and judgmental thoughts keep coming. Being Awake and Aware does not mean that all our thoughts must be pure, but it does require that we have none that we would keep. We don't need to analyze our fears just to let them go. Fears create blockages in our natural energy and result in pain and suffering: emotional and physical. The quicker our negative thoughts that are generated by fear are let go and replaced by positive thoughts, the sooner Awareness reappears.

The Buddha defined Enlightenment as the end of suffering. Constantly worrying about ourselves is suffering. We fear that we are not good enough or that we will fail. We feel people will turn on us, take advantage of us, or stop loving us. We have fear and we suffer from it. Problems occupy our minds, when one is solved the next one pops up. We listen to our minds which try to solve all our inner problems (eg. Fear) on the outside. This never solves the inner problem of not feeling whole and complete within ourselves. The key is to be quiet and accept the "what is" of life and keep our thoughts positive, loving, and peaceful. There is an ocean of LOVE behind all our fear and pain.

Our awareness of who we really are, the loved Son of God, is always present but is blocked by fear. We can always claim our "inner child" that has wonder, is joyful, spontaneous, and plays and lives in the present moment. Our Awareness is behind all thoughts and all experiences. It is in this Awareness that who we really are shines.

— CHAPTER THIRTEEN —
FORGIVENESS

If there were only one attribute to cultivate in order to lead a more spiritual life it would be Forgiveness. Forgiveness is generally misunderstood in our world. We think we are being forgiving when we forgive someone's bad behavior. After all, we must be the better person being able to forgive someone who has offended us.

Do we forgive our spouse if he or she has strayed from the marriage? Do we forgive a co-worker who has stepped over us for a promotion? Do we forgive a drunk driver who has killed our daughter? To forgive these behaviors is better than not forgiving. To carry resentment and blame is injurious to our physical and emotional health; it is so much better for us to release this burden through forgiveness.

But often this forgiveness comes with a judgment that what was done to us is really, really bad and the person who inflicted this pain on us is a bad person. But, since we think we are the better person we can prove this by forgiving someone who is obviously beneath us. The ego loves this type of forgiveness because it reinforces our feelings of separation from each other. We are the bigger person for forgiving such a terrible person or act.

With this type of forgiveness have we really forgiven, or are we just posturing and making ourselves feel better? There is a more profound Forgiveness that sets everyone free: the person who is forgiven and the one who forgives. This Forgiveness is based on the reality that nothing was ever really done to us. In truth we are a Spirit momentarily inhabiting a body in the illusion of this earth reality. Anything that was ever done to us was only done to our body in the dream and our Spirit remains totally intact with no injury. We can forgive what our brother never really did to us. We forgive the illusion that our bodies are who we are and are subject to eternal injury.

The body can hurt, so we think that any suffering the body experiences is real, whether physical or emotional. I know a father whose daughter was killed by a driver who strayed over the double yellow center line. The father was in enormous pain and did not deny that he was suffering. He also knew the greater reality that his daughter was OK, existing in a different dimension and that in this greater reality all was well. Within a few days he met with the driver who caused the crash that killed his daughter and her best friend and critically injured his wife; he offered Forgiveness. His Forgiveness was based on his wisdom of total Forgiveness that heals both parties. This was a great gift to himself and the driver. This Forgiveness allowed a healing for all involved.

Knowing that we are really Spirit allows us to feel the pain the body is experiencing and then let it go. Letting go lets us move into total and real Forgiveness holding nothing back, without feelings of separation. This has benefits for our Soul and also for our physical body. Judgmental forgiveness still hangs on to our emotional body as a superior feeling and is not healthy, while total Forgiveness lightens us up creating no emotional baggage. This type of complete Forgiveness is a way to freedom. Freedom from feeling isolated, alone, and separate from our fellow human beings, and it allows the feeling of connectedness to others. After all, we are all ONE and total Forgiveness recognizes what we do to others we do to ourselves. With this thought in mind, who are we really forgiving? In the greater reality there is no "other."

In a sense, Forgiveness is the final illusion that ends all illusions. Forgiveness is not required in Heaven because Heaven is non-dualistic. There is no subject or object in Heaven…therefore nothing to forgive. The world is dualistic, Heaven is singular.

— CHAPTER FOURTEEN —
JUDGMENT

"Judge not least you be judged." (Matthew 7:1–3). Two thousand years ago this was brought forth but it was never accepted by the general population. The same is true today. So many people live in the ego thought system where judgment plays a major role. It is part of the ego's blame game; others are responsible for my and the world's troubles. The ego loves comparisons. It does not matter to the ego if the judgment is putting someone else down or higher. Constantly comparing ourselves to others reinforces our separation from others, making us different from everyone else. Our original dream of being separate from God plays out here on the earth through the ego.

Of course, there is "good judgment." We are called to make choices all the time. For example, whether to cross the street against the light or spending the grocery money on the nag in the 5th race requires judgment. This type of judgment calls for discernment. It does not belittle anyone or anything. It is when the behavior of others, or even nature goes against us that we judge something as wrong and not acceptable to us.

Acceptance of "what is" is the key to non-judgment. This does not mean that we become door mats to negative behavior. We don't have to stay around people or things that are injurious to us. We can most likely leave the situation that is offending us without having to judge it as well. The problem with judging anything (that is, making it wrong or bad) is that it reinforces the ego thought system of separation.

What is the difference between judgment and observation? In both cases we observe behavior that has the potential to have us make a judgment, stating that this is wrong or bad. In observing such behavior, we simply notice it without an emotional response. We accept its existence and don't fall into the ego trap of making it wrong. This is often difficult because we are so used to judging that it is easy to make that person or situation wrong. The world around us is constantly judging and it is difficult not to join in.

Judgment does not just occur when things go against our wishes. Judgment also occurs when something we view as terrific occurs as well. Wise ones say that we should treat these two imposters as the same. When we judge that we are better than others, that too encourages the ego thoughts of separation.

Why are we so concerned with thoughts of separation, with the pride of the individual? The United States was built on individualism; the strength of the individual spirit. Isn't this what has made America great? It depends on your definition of "great." It certainly has helped make America the richest country in the world. But has it made the people the happiest? Annual United Nation polls show that the United States is not one of the happiest countries in the world. Their 2018 poll found the US in 18th position. That's 17 countries that are happier than we are. Has our economic success eliminated poverty, disease, mental illness, and suffering?

If our goal is to be better, richer, or healthier than the next guy, then judgment is a good tool to accomplish this. However, if our goal is to re-connect with that Divine spark within us, that spark that speaks of love, peace, gratitude, caring, and kindness, then judgment has no place in our lives. The great Spiritual truth is that we were created as the ONE Son of God. We are all One with God, so this apparent separation is not only not real, it keeps us from uniting back with our Creator and achieving joy while in the dream of our earthly life. Not judging, but accepting what is and forgiving all can lead to continued and unlimited happiness.

Differences often seem threatening to us. We grow up and exist in our own culture. For most of us it is transparent: We live in it without recognizing it as separate from our true selves. It is like a fish living in water without experiencing the water itself as separate. We often judge people that live in cultures different from ours. This keeps us separate from them. If we are fortunate enough to live in a completely different culture for a while, we begin to see that differing cultures are just a different expression of our One Self. It is like wearing a different outfit. Our bodies are the same no matter what clothes we are wearing although we appear different. We are all the same Self, Divine and connected no matter the external appearance.

— CHAPTER FIFTEEN —
GRATITUDE

Do we spend our time being grateful or complaining? Most of us would spend more time listing what is wrong with the world or wrong with people, or wrong with the events occurring in our lives. We often take for granted the good things and talk mostly about what's going wrong. Being the victim has its payoffs in gaining sympathy and attention from those around us. But it keeps us in the downward spiral of negativity. No matter what we do outside ourselves to fix what's wrong, problems seem to keep coming our way. That is because the "fix" is not outside us. Even if we solve specific negative events, the relief is only temporary as another problem presents itself.

The law of attraction postulates that the vibrations we send out attract like vibrations. If we are constantly complaining about how things are bad for us, that vibration attracts similar situations that are also negative. The form of our issue may change but the content (negativity) remains the same and continues to attract similar problems. And the solution to fixing all these issues lies within our Minds and not outside somewhere.

Practicing gratitude is a way out of this dilemma. At first it may be difficult to remember all the good things in our lives that we can be thankful for. It can be small things to start, like appreciating a sunny day, or a good meal, or a friend who stops by to say hello. The point is to keep our thoughts in the positive aspect of gratitude. The more we do this, the more we draw to us things to be grateful for. And we can even see beauty and good in most things we observe. It is our Minds that we need to keep in a good vibration because it is our Minds that create our reality.

— CHAPTER SIXTEEN —
CAUSE AND EFFECT

In this physical universe we all live by the universal law of cause and effect. For every action there is a reaction. We believe that when we see something we do not like, then a thought about it follows. We may have walked in a city and seen a beggar and then thought "what a sad world we live in where people don't have enough to eat." It may be surprising to learn that while there is cause and effect in this world they are reversed; for it is our thoughts that occur first and then what we perceive that follows. The cause is always our thought and the effect is what we experience.

This is also true with things that we see which we think are beautiful. We may see a young person helping an elderly person walk across the street, and then think people can be kind to one another. We erroneously believe that seeing that good deed generates our thought that people are kind. But this actually happens in reverse. If we are carrying thoughts that people are kind we are likely to see evidence that supports that belief. If we believe people are poor and suffering we will perceive situations that prove those beliefs.

Cause and effect happen so quickly that they occur almost simultaneously. It is easy to confuse which comes first: our thought or our perception. We create our own experiences by our thinking. This is why it is so important for us to discipline our mind. Don't tolerate negative thinking. When we catch ourselves thinking negatively, we need to change our mind. The quicker we can do this the quicker our life will change for the better. It takes practice.

Many teachers speak of "The Law of Attraction." What we are thinking creates a vibration which draws to us a like vibration. While the form that is drawn to us will most likely be different than our original thought, the content will be the same. That is, if we are thinking a negative thought about someone, we will be pulling other negative vibrations to us, although the actual form maybe something completely different; say, witnessing an auto accident. The good news is that if we discipline ourselves to continually move into positive thoughts, like vibrations of a positive nature will be pulled to us. Like to Like.

It is always our thought that comes first despite our temptation to believe that it is the other way around. Of course, this is not the way the world thinks. The world believes that events outside ourselves will cause how we think and feel. But everything we see is the result of our thoughts. Every thought we have brings either war or peace, fear or love, sadness or happiness. The world we see today has nothing to do with Reality. It is of our own making,

The world is actually a neutral place, neither good nor bad. But we don't have neutral thoughts. Our thoughts are either positive or negative. It is up to us to give meaning to the world, not the world to give meaning to us. We can always tell how we are thinking by how we feel. Negative thoughts make us feel bad and positive thoughts make us feel good. If we are feeling disturbed, sad, despondent, angry, fearful, anxious and the like, we can be sure that our thoughts have been negative. Keeping our thoughts positive generates a feeling of well-being.

If the less desirable events in the world are the effect of our thoughts, then it is our thoughts that need to be changed. Our Minds are mostly undisciplined and we are willing to think negatively. There is no point in lamenting the world or in trying to change the world with outside fixes. If we work on our problems in the world we may make some changes in the form, but underlying content will continue, perhaps in a different form. We are incapable of changing the content this way because the problem is merely an effect of our thinking. There is a point to changing our thoughts however because here we are changing the cause, and so the effect will change automatically.

The worldly person sees that problems are to be solved out there, while the spiritual person sees that the problems are to be solved within our own minds. While there may be some determination or fate in outer circumstances, but our experience of those circumstances are one of an inner decisions. Free will has to do with our attitudes which are totally under our control.

In each moment we have the power to create our own reality. Every thought results in form on some level. If we have peace and love in our hearts and in our thoughts, our life will be full of peace and love. When "negative" things seem to happen to us, we should look upon them as learning opportunities. We now have an opportunity to correct our thoughts and by so doing, to change our experience. The world is a big looking glass, reflecting back to us our thoughts at all times. Continually ask ourselves "What am I seeing? What am I thinking?" The world can be our teacher if we pay attention to what we are seeing and know that it is coming from our Mind.

We can be aware of our awareness and conscious of our consciousness. The more we are willing to let the world just be something we are aware of, the world ceases to be a problem. It is just something we are aware of and the more it will let us be who we really are: The Self, the Soul.

Peace of mind is an internal matter. Peace must begin with our own thoughts and then extend outward. It is from a peaceful

Mind that a peaceful perception of the world arises. It is better and more effective to change our Mind about the world than to try changing the outside world. It is not an error to work on changing the world, but if done while also changing our thoughts to Peace and Love and not judgment, the results will be lasting.

Remember, the Kingdom of Heaven is within, not without. The author of the book *King without a Kingdom* kept trying to find his Kingdom out in the world, and happiness kept eluding him because our real kingdom is not out there but within. One of Yeshua's main teachings was that the *"Kingdom of Heaven is Within."* Once we change our thoughts about the world, the world we see will change as well, to match our projections.

— CHAPTER SEVENTEEN —
EGO

The Ego was originally identified by Sigmund Freud (1856–1939) in his psychoanalytic theory which also included the Id and Superego. His definition of the Ego was the conscious mediator between the unconscious ID (childish & impulsive desires) and the unconscious Superego (judgmental and moralizing). The ego has come to mean a person's sense of self separate from the outside world. Considering oneself as distinct and separate from others and God is basic to the ego's thought system.

The thought system of separation we call the ego. This system of thought came into being when the One Son of God had a whim of what it might be like to be separate from God. Being created by God (LOVE) and being part of God, this was impossible. But the One Son of God believed separation from God was possible, and so began our dream of separation which resulted in the ego thought system and our universe of separate beings and things (the earth plane). Hallmarks of ego thinking are pride and self-importance about ourselves. Being a dream, the universe and the ego are simply illusions and are not real when compared to our True Reality, which is Heaven. Our egos are all about our individual self and not about the Spirits that we really are; the Self with a capital "S."

The ego thought system was created by us as a defense against our perceived notion that we had separated from God (impossible). Although in "True Reality" this separation never happened, we began our dream that it not only was possible, but actually happened. This powerful thought of separation created the dream of our entire universe, which has time and space and is based on dualism; day/night, love/fear, right/wrong, light/dark, man/woman, etc. The ego's very existence is based on this idea of separation and its middle name is "more."

When the One Son of God thought he had actually separated from God he felt tremendous Guilt. The ego's response was to have us leave our Mind for the physical world and to get separate bodies to focus us in the world. Humanity mirrors the duality found in the world that was made by the dreaming of the One Son of God. As individuals, we are a perishable physical element with a fragment of the Divine Essence; the Divine Spark. Most of us are ignorant of our Divinity within and only recognize our physical reality. Our egos keep us focused on our bodies and unaware of our Divine Essence and our ultimate destiny: to be re-united with God.

Many people think that the ego is necessary for humans to accomplish things in the world. This may be true. But the progress generated by the ego is not necessarily good at making mankind happier or more content. The ego loves competition with winners and losers. Competition can lead to technological innovation, which seemingly makes life on earth easier and better. But competition also reinforces the separation humans feel, one from another. The thought forms of separation are a hallmark of ego thinking and do not foster cooperation and caring for one another. The United States is a leader in technological innovation, yet rates poorly among other nations in the happiness of its citizens.

There was a man who wanted to rid himself of his ego. He spent the night in an underground Kiva, beating on a big bass drum and chanting for the ego to depart. All night long this chant continued, and by morning he was physically exhausted. His ego, however, was stronger than ever. He knew that he made up the ego so he should be able to get rid of it. But fighting it just strengthens it. Since the ego's very existence requires that we believe in separation, the way to reduce its influence on our lives is through Unity; viewing all of us as ONE. The more we dissipate our ego thoughts of separation, the less it has influence over us. And it is always up to us to choose that Divine aspect of ourselves over the ego in every situation.

We seek to know the world without really knowing ourselves.

"I am" this or that is the ego or the smaller "self."

"I" is the "Self" with a capital "S" and is who we really are.

The ego's voice is non-stop chatter all day long. It is running the show and never shuts up. It has commentary about everything. The ego's "ace in the hole" is that our bodies will always have problems whose solutions are out in the world, or so the ego believes. This roots our attention outside, where the ego lives, never inside us in our Minds, where the real solutions exist.

We have two aspects of our Mind; the Ego thought system and the Divine. We are the observer or the decision-maker and can choose between these two at any time. When an issue or a situation occurs, the ego usually speaks first and is the loudest, often taking our total attention. The Divine Spirit is softer and one needs to quiet the ego in order to hear it. It is like that comic depiction of the angel on one shoulder and the devil on the other, each speaking to us about what thought, word, or action is best. The problem is that that little devil is louder and more insistent.

The two voices are depicted in a Cherokee story of the grandfather and his grandson. The grandfather is telling his grandson of the fight that is occurring inside him between two wolves. One wolf is angry, greedy, judgmental, aggressive, and unkind. The other wolf is kind, peaceful, loving, caring, and accepting. The two wolves are having a great fight to the death. The grandson asks his grandfather, which wolf will win? The grandfather replied, the one you feed.

Part of the split mind believes in a personal self (ego), and if you give up this personal self your Mind will be healed. Only thoughts of Oneness, of love and peace, will exist in your Mind. All of your fear and your sense of lack and limitation comes from your belief that you are separate from God. Our Spirit cannot perceive and the ego cannot know. The psychologist, Carl Jung, tried to bring these opposites together. This is impossible, as they are mutually exclusive. The problem is that we are so identified with the ego thought system of separation that we think it is us and we don't know that we always have a choice to pick the Divine within our Minds.

Pain and suffering is caused by our resistance to "what is." This pain is the dark shadow cast by the ego. The ego wants its identity to prevail and it lives in our Fears and Guilt. The ego is concerned with control, not wholeness, which must be hidden in order to protect the ego's existence. But the ego is made up by us, so we have the power to eliminate it; not by fighting it, but by ignoring its calls for revenge, blame, and judgment, and listening to our Divine thought system of forgiveness, love, and kindness in all situations.

Our problems are never external. The problem is always that we have chosen the ego thought system to deal with our pain. The ego doesn't really want our problems solved, for our perceived problems are what keeps it alive. The ego created a problematic world in order to protect us from God and wants to keep us unaware that we can make the choice between our Divinity, our right mind of peace, love, and caring, rather than the ego thoughts of blame, judgment, revenge, greed, etc. The ego wants to keep us mindless so we can't choose differently. The word "ego" should not even be used since it does not exist, except in the illusion.

We are unaware of the power of our Minds. The nature of LOVE is to extend itself. That is creation. Man, through his ego mis-creates. Man projects. God extends.

The ego is an impediment to God Realization and also dampens one's life. It identifies itself through the physical body and is limited to the five senses. It is a dark covering around the Soul and it blocks the flow of grace from God. One cannot fight the ego, as direct confrontation only strengthens it. Having the discipline and taking the time to listen to the Divine side of our minds rather than the ego slowly dissolves it. Give the ego no attention and it will disappear. Practicing a loving response to all situations that arise reduces the ego within us. Being more and more in the present moment, rather than in the past or future, also reduces the ego's influence in our lives because the ego does not exist in the Now.

Why do we normally choose the ego thought system rather than the Divine? It is because we have identified with the dream here and do not want to wake up and possibly lose our individual identity. We would rather bring Yeshua and God into our dream than Awake from the dream. This is promulgated by the Christian Church. Yet God is unaware of our dream, the illusion of the earth plane. The ego likes to think we can bring God into our dream, as it traps us in the dream. The goal is to Awaken from the dream, not continue it.

Yeshua, during his year-long ministry 2,000 years ago, was completely without ego. After his baptism by John the Baptist, his ego departed and he had a direct link to his Higher Self and to God. This did not make him the "only Son of God" to the exclusion of everyone else as Christianity proclaims. Yeshua is just like us, but perhaps an older brother who has re-united with the God within and is an example for us. Yeshua is due our love and devotion because he is a model for our complete Awareness of God in our life, which is still only a potential in us.

Being "Spiritual" could be defined as the absence of our egos. The ego can be defined as our thought forms of separation;

separation from God, each other, and all other forms. Spirituality is best pursued in the daily challenges of ordinary living. This is an individual quest; a journey without distance. Inner peace and LOVE is our natural state and lies within all of us. Its access is through the present moment; the Now, which is truly our only existence. It cannot be by thinking, only through experience, which is unable to be adequately described in words.

— CHAPTER EIGHTEEN —
RELIGION

Yeshua, two thousand years ago, had no intention of creating a religion. He was teaching the Jewish scriptures in a new and impactful way using his great charisma, lack of ego, healing abilities, and storytelling through parables. His only new message was that "the Kingdom of Heaven is within" and to "Love your neighbor AND your enemies." These ideas were new to the land of Judea, and not even the Essene community, who we regard as spiritually advanced, embraced these ideas. It was after Yeshua dropped his body that Paul, who had never met or seen Yeshua, with his relentless travels and letters, promoted a new "Christian" religion. It was not Yeshua.

22% of Americans believe that Yeshua is coming back in the next 50 years. Another 22% believe Yeshua will come back some day. 30 million members of 45,000 churches believe the Bible to be the infallable, authoritative word of God. The "second coming of Christ" is our inner awareness of our God essence; It is Christ's return within us.

An example of how man wrote the Bible comes from Luke and Mark:

Luke 12:10

"And whosoever shall speak a word against the Son of man, it shall be forgiven him: but unto him that blasphemeth against the Holy Ghost it shall not be forgiven."

Mark 3:29

"But he that shall blaspheme against the Holy Ghost hath never forgiveness, but is in danger of eternal damnation."

Yeshua's message was always one of LOVE and Forgiveness. Never non-forgiveness or eternal sin. LOVE does not judge or condemn.

It seems that The Lord's Prayer has also been misunderstood:
"…Thy kingdom come
Thy will be done
On Earth as in Heaven …"

Yeshua was constantly requested to immerse himself into world affairs, to lead the Jewish people out of Roman domination and to rule the world. Yeshua made it clear that the Kingdom is within us not necessarily to be created out in the world. He never dealt with correcting matters of the material world other than to say *"Give unto Caesar what is Caesar's."* Even Yeshua's statement of *"Those without sin throw the first stone,"* was about inner awareness, not about criminal law. The Lord's Prayer is calling for us on Earth to recognize our **inner kingdom** with God…as it is in Heaven.

In the last 2,000 years religion has been the cause of most of the wars and killings. Human beings are alone in the animal kingdom as to the mass slaughter of their fellow human beings. In the last century alone over 100 million of our fellows have been murdered by us. No other species kills its own kind in such numbers. It seems that most religions are based on a prophet who speaks of the universal wisdom of LOVE and not hate and killing. Yet historically it is the separation thoughts of one religion versus another religion (which must be wrong) that has been the cause of so much killing. In the past the Crusades and the Inquisition are examples of this willingness to kill those who worship in a different way. In the present, Jihad is an example of this same willingness to kill those who worship the one God in a different way. But God is too big to be housed in only one religion. The Persian poet Rumi (1207–1273), when speaking of the Islamic religion stated, "The Light of Mohammed does not abandon a Zoroastrian or a Jew. May the shade of His good fortune shine upon everyone."

Most organized religions feel that theirs is the true way to God and often the only way to God. Wars over whose God is the right one have been fought over the centuries.

One newer religion, The Baha'i Faith (1863), attempts to incorporate all religions. Based on the teachings of Bahá'ulláh (1817–1892), the Baha'i Faith believes in universal peace as the supreme goal of mankind. Baha'is are focused on personal and societal transformation. They also believe in the oneness of the entire human race and the basic unity of all religions. According to the Baha'is, walking a path of service to God and to humanity gives life meaning and prepares one for the moment the soul separates from the body and continues on its eternal journey toward its maker. Even with their universal message, the Baha'is have a history of being persecuted by followers of Islam.

While the transgressions of organized religion are legion, millions have found peace and comfort in their religions. Based on a core of spiritual truths, there is a foundation of teachings that lift us up. "Perennial Wisdom" is the common core underlying all the world's great religions. While most religious rituals have been dissociated from their original purpose and have lost their real meaning, the Muslim practice of praying to God five times a day is one ritual that is effective in keeping Muslims in touch with God. Meher Baba stated that "The way of the path is made of Love not rituals." Going to church, temple, mosque, or any spiritual place is valuable if inner peace is the result. The challenge is to escape the dogma and the belief that only our religion is the right and only path to God. This attitude only serves to separate us, one from another, and unity is lost.

There are many religions and sub-groups, but most scholars consider that there are 12 classical world religions. They are listed below with a very approximate estimate of their followers.

Christianity	2,000,000,000
Islam	1,500,000,000
Hinduism	1,000,000,000
Buddhism	480,000,000
Shinto	100,000,000
Sikhism	30,000,000
Judaism	15,000,000
Baha'i Faith	8,000,000
Jainism	5,000,000
Zoroastrianism	130,000
Taoism*	
Confucianism*	

Note: *Taoism and Confucianism both originated in China and both have been banned by the current Chinese government. Therefore, numbers of followers are difficult to estimate, but it would certainly be in the hundreds of millions.

While most avatars and mystics had no impulse to create a religion based on their teachings, most followers found it necessary to form an organization around their master's teachings in order to preserve them. This is mostly an expression of the ego's need for control and power and the resulting organization often puts a barrier between us and God. One needs a priest or holy man to intercede between us and God. Direct experience of God without the dogma and rituals of an organized religion are frowned upon, if not outright punishable by death. It is my opinion that Enlightenment never came from following the rules of a religion.

Christianity was created by men who lived hundreds of years after Yeshua. It is doubtful that if Yeshua were alive today that he would recognize the Church as based on his teachings. He would wonder why women seemed to be in second place, not only in Christianity but also in other religions as well. Christianity has tried to bring God's light into the dream rather taking the dream to the Light. That is, we want God to come into our earthly lives to solve our earthly problems. This makes no sense if our earthly lives are but a dream. Does one try to enter their child's dream to make the dream better or do we gently awaken our child from a troubling dream? Since most of us don't want to leave the dream and our individual identity, most of us are afraid of the Light (God's LOVE) in that it will release us from the dream, and our personal identities.

Yeshua would not have felt one needed a church in order to find God; quite the opposite. In the Gospel of Thomas, discovered near Nag Hammadi in Upper Egypt in 1945, Yeshua was reported as saying *"...the kingdom is inside of you. When you come to know yourselves then you will become known, and you will realize that this is who you are, the son of the living father. But if you will not know yourselves you dwell in poverty."* In the Nag Hammadi Gospel of Thomas there are no miracles, no prophecy, no ending of the world, no dying for one's sins, and no crucifixion. In Truth, we are ALL part of the One Son of God and our Awareness of who we really are is the True and only Reality. Thomas Aquinas stated some 800 years ago, "To one who has faith no explanation is necessary. To one without faith, no explanation is possible."

During the two hundred years after Yeshua departed the earth plane there were many small groups centered around the teachings of Yeshua. Even in these early days there was disagreement as to how and what to worship. The first book (Mark) of the New Testament was not put together until 60-plus years after Yeshua's death. The books of Mathew and Luke were composed 15 to 20 years later. And the other books followed even later. None of the Books of Mathew, Mark, Luke, and John were actually written by the disciples but were put together by other writers. Interestingly,

Pope Leo (1475–1521) has been quoted as saying that "the fable of Christ has served our company very well."

Some Christian scholars feel that about 25% of what the Bible has Yeshua saying is true. The balance has been grossly expanded or made up completely. And the descriptions of his life have been enhanced and expanded by New Testament authors often to correspond to previous predictions or historical interpretations. Conversely, The Gospel of Thomas is full of Yeshua's sayings that are mostly accurate.

The Gnostic Christians were active in those early years. Their name, Gnostics, came from the Greek word Gnosis, meaning knowledge. This knowledge was meant to be acquired through personal religious experience not through words. "Sophia" or wisdom, recognizes the Divine Spark in man, derived from God. Man fell into this world of fate, birth, and death and needs to be awakened to the Divine part of our split mind—our Self.

The Gnostics celebrated the wisdom of all sacred texts from all religions. They found wisdom in the Tao, Buddhism, Zoroastrianism, Hellenic Greece, Hinduism, ancient Egypt, Jewish Scriptures, and in more recent times, Islam and included their wisdom into their beliefs. They valued and included woman as Yeshua did. They believed that God existed inside ALL of us as taught by Yeshua. There was no need for priests as intermediaries between us and God and that we could find God on our own, without a church.

Gnostics viewed the world as flawed, as do all religions, but differ in the concept of why it is flawed and what to do about it. According to the Gnostics, the world was not created by God, but by lesser forces. This is similar to the "One Son of God" who had a whim of what it might be like to be separate from God (as described in *A Course in Miracles*). The concept of Original Sin comes from the One Son of God thinking that it would be possible to be separate from God. The Adam and Eve story is based on this as well. It seems to make sense that God, **who is only LOVE**, could NOT make a world of disease, war, poverty, pain, greed, sadness, etc., but we, as the One son of god, made this dream Universe through our egoic thoughts of separation after we believed that we could leave God and be separate.

In the Gnostic view, there is a true, ultimate, and transcendent God who is beyond all created universes and who never created anything in our dream universe. God did bring forth from within Himself the substance of all there is in all the worlds, visible and invisible. It may be true then that all is God, for all consists of the substance of God. It must also be recognized that many portions of the Divine essence have been projected so far from their source that they are not Divine. Gnostics believed in non-attachment to the world; "being in the world but not of the world." Most people today could not abide such a concept as non-attachment since we are in such a state of materialistic desires. Gnostics also believed in a lack of egotism, a respect for all beings, and experiencing the knowledge of the heart rather than words and concepts.

The Gnostics challenged the authority of priests and bishops because they believed one should embrace God directly. The fathers of the new Christian church proclaimed that there was only one way to find God an that was through believing that Yeshua was the ONLY Son of God. Only through the mediation of priests could one find the one true God.

At the end of the second century, Bishop Irenaeus of Lyon insisted that the four gospels of Mathew, Mark, Luke, and John were to be the only dogma of the church—only these four, and that all the other gospels floating around at the time, including those eventually found at Nag Hammadi, were to be destroyed. Bishop Irenaeus justified keeping only four gospels because he felt there were only four corners of the universe and only four principal winds. When these four gospels became the official dogma of the church, all others were to be destroyed, and any followers of those other gospels were to be persecuted and branded heretics. It was all about control in the early Christian church as they felt they needed to control their followers. The Church became an institution of man.

Eventually the Gnostic Christians were condemned as heretics by the Christians following Paul's teachings, and most of their books and teachings were destroyed. When this happened the Gnostics hid the writings of the apostles that were not of the four adopted by the Church (Mathew, Mark, Luke, and John). Fragments of the other gospels were found but it was not until 1945 that a Bedouin unearthed a previously hidden cache of 50 ancient papyrus texts at a location in upper Egypt called Nag Hammadi. Only a few people took note of this discovery. These ancient texts slipped into obscurity and were not opened or translated from their original Coptic texts until more recent times.

From the translation of these ancient texts came the "secret teachings' of Yeshua know as the four Gnostic Gospels:

"The Secret Book of James"
"The Gospel of Thomas"
"The Book of Thomas"
"The Secret Book of John"

These apostles were known as Gnostics. They believed that God exists within everyone and the way to God was through the wisdom of self knowledge, through gnosis.

The Gnostics were close to the actual teachings of Yeshua but they did not form a church and were overshadowed, dismissed, and branded heretics by the emerging Christian Church that was based on the teachings of Paul. It seems to me that the Christian Church fell prey to the ego of man.

The fact that many religions, at their core, share universal truths is demonstrated by how the "Golden Rule" appears in different religions.

Christianity

"In everything do to others as you would have done to you." Mathew 7:12

Islam

"None of you truly believes until he desires for his brother what he desires for himself."

Prophet Muhammad

Hinduism

"Do not do to others what would cause pain if done to you." Mahabharata 5:1517

Buddhism

"Treat no other in ways that you yourself would find hurtful." Udana-Vargas 5.18

Judaism

"What is hateful to you do not do to your neighbor. This is the whole Torah. All the rest is commentary." Talmud: Shabbat 3 ia

If only these universal sayings were followed by the world, it would be transformed.

— CHAPTER NINETEEN —
RESURRECTION

If Yeshua wasn't crucified, then there was no resurrection. Yet the crucifixion and bodily resurrection of Yeshua is a critical belief of the Christian Church. Without it, a main tenant of its doctrine would be gone along with many of its adherents. As was examined earlier, resurrection was a common attribute of many previous "gods" in history. This is because the actual process of resurrection has been practiced over many millennia.

The Biblical story of Lazarus was in fact a three-day process of resurrection where the body lies in state while the soul travels through different dimensions and then returns with a wider awareness of the spiritual domain. From the outside it would appear that the person in such a three-day state is actually dead, but he is like in a coma while he travels. Yeshua did not raise the dead, but simply awakened Lazarus when his three-day journey was completed. When Yeshua was baptized by John the Baptist, it was a form of resurrection in that he emerged from the water without an ego and had a clear connection to his Higher Self and the Holy Spirit.

The Christian Church has made the resurrection of Yeshua all about the resurrection of his physical body. And some

Christian sects believe that we will keep our bodies after death. If we were created in the image of God, which I believe is true, then who we are is Spirit, not a body. Our soul is greater and larger than our bodies and after we drop our bodies, our soul continues. There is no death of our Spirit. Resurrection then is a process of reconnecting to our Higher Self, our Soul, our Spirit. Traditional resurrection has us laying our bodies aside for a few days to journey as our Spirit into higher vibrational dimensions in order to widen our perspective and release our ties to the material world. It frees us from the bonds of materialism.

The Great Pyramid of Giza was built many thousands of years ago for the purpose of resurrection. The Kings chamber and the sarcophagus was not a burial chamber for Pharos, but an energy enhancing space to allow a three-day journey into other dimensions. The process of resurrection has been a tool for mystics and avatars for centuries. The three-day period comes from the Winter Solstice where the sun, our day-star, stops for three days and then starts its rebirth into greater light. This auspicious time was coopted by the Christian writers as Yeshua's birthday as did many other godly figures from history. The sun has been a symbol of rebirth and resurrection for thousands of years.

While we may not be comfortable to experience a three-day resurrection or even have the right place to experience such an event, we can mimic the process through meditation. A ten-day Vipassana meditation can create a space for a personal resurrection. Or even daily meditation can allow us to experience the silence and wonder of a vibration quite different from earth. We need not incur a physical journey to Awakening since, as Yeshua stated, the Kingdom is not out there someplace but within. The journey back to God is a journey without distance.

— CHAPTER TWENTY —

SICKNESS

Is sickness all in the mind? It sure doesn't feel so when we are suffering. Hardly anyone consciously wants to be sick. But what about unconscious desires that are transparent to our conscious minds? There are payoffs for one to be sick: being a victim, gaining an identity, receiving sympathy from others, being excused from work, and evading a stressful situation, to name a few. A famous health practitioner from Australia always tests new clients first, using applied kinesiology (muscle testing) prior to treating their illness to determine if they really want healing. Often, the subconscious prefers the illness for many of the reasons stated earlier. In this case almost all healing modalities will be ineffective.

Allopathic medicine can often reduce or eliminate the symptoms of an illness. But pain is often useful to us, as it can be a signal to get back to our Minds, where the real change can take place. One can keep using medication but we may miss a turning point in our lives where we decide against the ego and sickness and claim the divinity of our Minds. What we consider is wrong in the world and in our bodies is actually what is going on in our Minds.

Stress is a major underlying cause for many illnesses. Stress is resisting life's events, not the events themselves. Acceptance of "what is" helps us to avoid this resistance. We still deal with events in our life but we allow them to be and then let them pass on through. Avoiding issues that stress us only pushes them down into the unconscious and they will need to be dealt with at some future time. It is best to acknowledge our issue, feel it, and then let it go. There are numerous workshops and books that can help us deal successfully with eliminating stress in our life. For those who want a healthy, happy life, anything we can do to eliminate stress will yield major benefits. But our efforts need to be directed within, not to try and change the outside circumstances. Life's issues, one after another, will always be there for us so it is imperative that we change our Mind to acceptance rather than dealing outside with the problem. It is true that sometimes outside circumstances need to be dealt with head on, but the cure to stress is always an inside job. The **worldly** person tries to solve his or her problems "out there." The **aware** person solves their problems within their Minds.

All of us come into the earth plane with samskaras (a Sanskrit word meaning "impressions") picked up from previous incarnations. This is one of the main reasons for our willingness to reincarnate, to deal with these impressions and hopefully eliminate them. They are an unfinished energy pattern that can run our life. Energy naturally expands outward, and when we stop it, it circles around like a planet around the sun and stays stored in the heart chakra, causing blockages to our Awareness. The key is to always let our problems go through Forgiveness.

If life seems confusing it is because WE are confused, not because life is confusing. What gives life meaning is the willingness to live it. Have no preferences. Remain centered in the Tao; the peace of acceptance. Nothing is personal. When in pain we need to just feel the edges, but avoid going there to stay. Be in the center, in the Tao.

In the big picture all disease is an illusion because it is a body thing, and the body is part of the illusion that is our world. Due to the state of our earth plane that is ego driven, it can be difficult to stay healthy. The ego loves sickness because it seemingly makes the body real, which is the home of the ego. We tend to buy into the seeming reality of chaos, sickness, greed, poverty, sadness, war, etc. In Reality we are the One Son of God, perfect and LOVED unconditionally. This is an **affirmation** that needs to be stated, not only in the early morning and at night before we retire, but all through the day. Stay Aware of who we really are. *"I am not a body, I am free. I am still as God created me."* Relax into the knowing that we are LOVED by God and our Spirit is totally protected.

— CHAPTER TWENTY-ONE —

SUFFERING

If we scratch below the surface of peoples' outward expressions of normalcy, we often find some form of suffering. It seems everyone is carrying some unhappiness or misery, or some problem that has their attention. Henry David Thoreau in his book *Walden*, stated that "most men lead lives of quiet desperation." Almost all suffering is caused by resistance to the "what is." The resultant pain is the dark shadow cast by the ego. Since we are the ones who created the ego, we are also able to dispense with it. Not by fighting it directly, but by being in the present and accepting the "what is." The ego does not exist in the Now, only in our dwelling in the past or the future. Giving the ego no attention it will wither away and cease its control over us.

The present moment is our only reality and the only place where change can be made. What happens in the moment cannot be undone, because it already is. Surrender is an active state that allows solutions from our Higher Self to come forward. It is up to us to live in a state of non-resistance to those things that we think make us suffer. We often go to pseudo escape which is only temporary and eventually makes things worse: work, alcohol, drugs, anger, projection, or suppression.

At the level of Being, all suffering is recognized as an illusion. Since suffering is due to the identification with form and since form only exists within the illusion of our world, the way out of suffering is to identify with the greater reality of LOVE. ACIM states *"Nothing real can be threatened. Nothing unreal exists. Herein lies the peace of God."* Healing comes from the recognition that spiritual energy creates no suffering for us, or others, or any life form on this planet.

Stress is caused by being here but wanting to be somewhere else. The ego will try to keep us trapped in time, because that is the foundation of its very existence. It is in the past or future where our problems lie, not in the present. Our internal watcher is beyond form. When consciousness is directed outward the world arises but when directed inward it becomes its own Source.

One can heal through "Being" rather than by doing anything. Resistance to our problems is weakness and fear masquerading as strength. Surrender is an inner acceptance of "what is" without any reservation. Surrender does not mean doing nothing. It is not resignation. Surrender does not transform "what is" directly, but transforms us internally, and when that happens our whole world is transformed. This is true because the outer world is but a reflection of our inner world.

When our consciousness is directed outward the world arises. When consciousness is directed inward it realizes its own Source. Enlightenment cannot be grasped by thinking about it. It is experienced in the present only, not in the past or in the future. And the experience is most difficult to explain or describe. Our inability to feel our inner connection to God gives rise to the illusion of separateness from our Self and the world around us. And this always involves some sort of suffering. Suffering is an internal choice about what to feel about the things we think we observe out there.

We need to remember that we are the observer of the voices in our heads and can make choices as to what to think and experience. When we are able to observe our Mind we are not trapped within it. All problems are illusions of the Mind, which the ego loves as it gives us our identity. It is simply that if we get the inside right, the outside will fall into place.

There is no form of suffering that fails to hide an unforgiving thought. Forgiveness is a way out of suffering because nothing can touch the radiant essence of who we really are.

— CHAPTER TWENTY-TWO —
ACTIVISM

Does the earth's dramatic environmental destruction now taking place require us to engage in activism to help save our planet? Do the ills of the world—poverty, greed, war, inequality, suffering, etc.—require us to engage in solving all our myriad of problems?

The planet is certainly undergoing an extreme environmental degradation. Our human ecological footprint is expanding. Today 2.7 billion people face water scarcity. We annually use over 150% of the earth's capacity of renewable resources. Eighty percent of the earth's forests have been destroyed and this is continuing at the rate of 78 million acres per year. This is significant as over 13% of global carbon emissions come from deforestation.

Coral reefs are disappearing at twice the rate of forest destruction. The average ocean temperature has risen over 2 degrees Celsius, which doesn't seem like much, but in the ocean it is causing major harm. To coral reefs it is akin to a human body's temperature rising by the same amount. Consider the damage that would cause to our bodies. One fifth of our coral reefs have been destroyed by warming seas and overfishing. Scientists estimate that another 35% could die in the next 10 to 40 years. This may be a conservative estimate as coral reefs can die very quickly since they are sensitive to the smallest change in water temperature. This will have a serious impact on the marine environment, since 25% of all marine life is connected in some way to the coral reefs. The ocean is the major carbon sink on earth, making the ocean waters more acidic and less hospitable to sea life. The oceans are also the earth's heat sink, taking 92% of the earth's atmospheric warming created by the expanding blanket of carbon in the air. If this warming went exclusively to the land mass, the earth's average temperature would be 122^0 F. If the oceans go, the earth goes too.

The extreme extent of species loss has been well reported by the scientific community. While there is a natural evolution in species dying and being replaced, extinctions are now occurring faster than ever before. Earth is in the midst of a mass extinction of life. Scientists estimate that 150 to 200 species of plant, insect, bird, fish, and animal become extinct every day. Many biologists believe this level of extinction is greater than anything the world has experienced since the vanishing of the dinosaurs nearly 65 million years ago.

While politicians argue as to the cause of this degradation and even its existence, scientists are almost unanimous in agreeing the cause is due to human activity: abuse of our natural resources or carbon emissions. We are tempted to put our attention to solving these problems out in the world, to change the system or to change the way humans live. While this type of activism can be effective to a degree, alone it will never solve our environmental and social challenges.

A large chapter of GreenPeace located outside the United States was looking to create a new headquarters. They hired an individual to facilitate the design and location for their new building by working with all the department heads over several meetings. The facilitator agreed to this job, as he was impressed with the work of this environmental organization. To his surprise and dismay, he noticed that the members of this group as individuals were neither green nor peaceful. Full ash trays, used coffee cups piled high near the sink, and leftover donuts on the table were not indicative of a green lifestyle. There were heated arguments and turf wars over facilities and design, with disparaging remarks against fellow workers that did not speak well of peace being a major personal consideration. It is often easier to try to correct imbalances outside our self than it is to attend to our own personal state of physical health and emotion. The facilitator could only imagine the increased effect of this organization if the individuals were also green and peaceful in their personal endeavors as well.

Sages and mystics mainly agree that changing our inner landscape to Love, Peace, and Harmony is the way to effect change in the world. It is often stated that an Awake person, through his presence only, can affect 10,000 beings positively without any word or outward action. Ramana Maharshi wisely stated "Your own Self-realization is the greatest service you can render to the world." If our inner world is one of LOVE, our outward behavior will be kind, caring, and of service. Leaving the ego behind and using Forgiveness of not only our adversaries but of the whole world condition is the best way to create change. From this base, activism can be very powerful.

There is a very intelligent man who is active in his small community to bring about a more just society. He brings well-thought-out arguments to support moving the town to a more equitable and compassionate state. I believe, however, that his impact in the community, while considerable, is more to do with his open and caring heart which people respond to. If his approach were anger and condemnation he would not get the audiences he receives and his effect would be limited. Unless the ego thoughts of separation are eliminated or vastly reduced, progress towards a more equitable and caring community will be limited. It is a sad state when even "peace" marches often turn to violence. One activist recently stated that he no longer participates in "peace" marches because they are too dangerous.

Giving service to others is our essential means for awakening. Service need not be a sacrifice, which can breed resentment. What we do for others we also do for ourselves; we are all part of the One.

There are several new organizations sprouting up that combine a loving essence and a program to deal with the ills of this world and this is very encouraging. One such emerging group is Economic Democracy Advocates (EDA). This is a growing international group promoting an alternative economic system (PROUT) to a capitalist system, which unfettered has resulted in inequality, poverty, and earth degradation due to the economic and political control by the corporate oligarchy now in power. At EDA's core is the acceptance that we are all One and that what we do to each other we do to ourselves. Unlike Communism, which had wonderful ideals but resulted in dictator-type controls over human life, EDA proposes a more local and regional control of the economy allowing for differences in needs and capabilities. A more participatory community is envisaged that allows for easy communication of ideas and programs that benefit all. But before any system can change, the hearts and minds of the people must change first. A new system overlaid on existing ego thoughts of "me first" will just not succeed.

How can we make these necessary changes to our economic and social systems that will save our planet and enhance life on earth? It must begin with our own inner balance; choosing our Divine thoughts of LOVE and Peace in ALL situations and to ignore the incessant voice of the ego to blame, get even, and take care of only ourselves at the expense of everyone and everything else.

There are many paths to help us achieve this inner peace, this Love of ourselves and our fellow humans as well as all the other life forms existing on our planet. There are so many good paths up the mountain that one can barely see the mountain itself. This is good news, as we all have different backgrounds, beliefs, and proclivities so that only one path or religion cannot begin to serve all of us. In the main, it is an individual effort to achieve an Awakened state of Mind. It is the only way to achieve our Inner Peace and to pass that onto the world at large. As Yeshua stated some 2,000 years ago, the real Kingdom is within, not without.

— CHAPTER TWENTY-THREE —
AWARENESS

Awareness is the state of being present and can be considered synonymous with Enlightenment. It is the overwhelming presence of Love, which is the basis of our Universe. Awareness is always present although it can be blocked or hidden by our thoughts and experiences. Awareness is who we are. It is a state beyond time and space and it is what actually experiences our bodies, our thoughts, and our life events. Our Awareness is clouded over when we get so caught up in our bodies, events, and thoughts that we believe this is who we are.

"The unexamined life is not worth living" (Socrates, 469–399 BCE). We most often seek to know the world rather than know ourselves. Gnothi sauton, "Know Yourself," is inscribed at the entrance to the holy shrine of Apollo at Delphi in Greece. This ancient saying has been used in Greek, Christian, and Gnostic thought. In the Gospel of Thomas, the Gnostic Coptic texts found at Nag Hamadi in upper Egypt in 1945, Yeshua is quoted as saying *"Rather the kingdom is inside you and outside you. When you know yourself then you will be known...But if you do not know yourself, then you live in poverty and embody poverty"* In the Book of Thomas, also part of the Gnostic writings, Yeshua stated *"For whoever does not know self does not know anything, but whoever knows self already has acquired knowledge about the depth of the universe."* Knowing self is knowing the spirit or the divine light withn.

"Awareness" or "Being" can be felt as the ever present "I Am." Being cannot be knowable through the brain and only experienced. Any attempt to describe it fails because it is beyond the human brain. The "Second Coming" is simply our returning to our consciousness; free from the illusion that we are a body. Enlightenment is awakening from the dream; only a recognition, not a change at all.

Awareness of who we really are, the Loved Son of God, is always present but can be blocked and hidden by our fearful thoughts. Our thoughts seem incessant, but don't despair their seemingly unstoppable rampage. Being Aware does not mean all thoughts must be pure and positive, but it does require that there are no thoughts that we would keep. The quicker the negative thoughts generated by fear are let go by replacing them with more positive thoughts the more Awareness can be accessed. "Just Say No to Negativity" was a recent, funny, bumper sticker. But it is ALL thoughts (positive and negative) and ALL experiences that are blocking our Awareness. This is because, while thoughts and experiences seem real and who we are, this is just not the case. We identify ourselves with our thoughts and experiences rather than our Awareness of Love.

Awareness accepts the "what is" in our thoughts and experiences but knows that is not who we really are. Who is the experiencer? Who is the observer? Is it our personality? Or is it our Mind beyond the brain, beyond the physical, beyond time and space. Come to know the One who watches and we will know one of the great mysteries of creation. Life's events may be pre-determined, but our inner life and all our attitudes are open and controllable by our free will. Be aware of our

Awareness. Be conscious of our Consciousness. The more we are willing to let the world just be, something we are aware of, the more it will let us Be who we really are, our True Self, with a capital "S." We are not a human being, we are just watching one.

— CHAPTER TWENTY-FOUR —

DEATH AND REINCARNATION

Everything in our illusory world reincarnates and goes through the evolution of incarnation, birth, and death. The flow is consistent, never ending and exacting. Each lifetime is a step towards another vibration or dimension within the physical plane. There is reincarnation within mineral, plant, animal, and within atom and molecule. There is a level of consciousness within each.

In our illusory universe reincarnation takes place in the constellations, the solar system, planets, our earth, the sun, the microcosm, and of course, us. When the energy of a constellation has fulfilled its vibrational force and its magnitude has grown to brilliance unknown to us, then it is ready to be replaced by another. The solar system vibrates and feels the pressures of all its underlying energies of planetary force. It too can reincarnate to constellation and planet to solar system, and perhaps, us to planet. Few see this big. It is difficult to imagine vastness when we are lost within our small self.

Death releases us and our divine spark from the lowly prison of identification with the material earth plane and our body. While in our earthly life, if we have not Awakened sufficiently from the physical reality, it is likely that our Divine spark will reincarnate into another body once again. We love our personal identity and return to earth to re-experience our individual separateness. The transcendental knowledge and experience that we have come from a Divine Reality must come to us while we are still in a body here on earth or reincarnation becomes inevitable.

Death does not automatically bring liberation and those of us who have not attained a liberating knowledge of who we really are while we are embodied on earth are most likely trapped once more into bodily existence through reincarnation.

Most people are so identified with their body that they fear death. Are we a human having a spiritual experience or a Spirit having a human experience? Our infinite Self is Spirit, not a body. In that regard there is no death as our Spirit continues forever and ever. When the weather changes from winter to summer and we take off our coat do we lament the loss of our coat? Even if we lose our coat, we can always secure another. It is the same with our body.

Those who believe in an afterlife most often believe in heaven and hell. We go to one or the other when we die. And both are located someplace else, away from the earth. Yet, when we drop our bodies most of us exist in a different dimension we could call the "spirit world." This realm is not heaven or hell but consists of a different reality still connected to the earth plane. Here we review our past life, and with much greater perception we determine, by ourselves but with some guidance, what we accomplished and what karma we created. God is not judgmental and there is no judgment coming from Him. We judge ourselves with great clarity of what we wanted to accomplish in this past life and how we did. This is not a negative process, but more of a learning exercise.

There is great support from other Spirits in the spirit world and one feels loved and acknowledged. Guidance is all around, positive and beneficial. We begin to feel what lessons and situations we would like to experience next and with what other Spirits we wish to experience the earth plane. We often come back to the earth with groups of souls that we have incarnated with before.

As we create our own reality on the earth plane with our thoughts, so too in the spirit world do we create our own experience. The spirit world is not heaven but is part of the physical plane. This dimension has a myriad of levels and one goes to the vibration where we most resonate. If we have specific beliefs of what it will be like that is most likely what we will perceive, at first. So, if we believe only Mormons go to heaven, when we pass into the spirit realm we will only see other Mormons and we will believe that we are in heaven. If we believe that we are going to hell when our body drops, the spirit world will seem like our idea of what hell is. Spirit guides help us discern a more accurate reality and we begin to release all of these pre-conceived notions of what and where we think we are.

Some souls are reluctant to return to the earth plane. In the spirit world we remember all our past lives and we feel much larger than our limited immediate past life. The spirit world is so much more expansive than the earth, and it is full of love and light. We begin to realize, however, that it is only on the earth plane where the lessons we wish to experience and learn can take place.

While we return to Earth to work on lessons we feel we need to learn, we often incur additional samskaras or karma while living on the earth that we feel requires another lifetime to address. Thus, the karmic wheel continues with life after life until we Awaken from the dream. Many sages feel that we have millions of lifetimes before we release all karma and evolve out of this seemingly endless cycle and leave the spirit world, returning to heaven. Others feel we have only 9 to 12 lifetimes in which to complete our cycle on earth. Since there is no time in Reality, how many lifetimes in the dream we have is irrelevant to our real existence.

There is no time in the spirit world realm, therefore there is no sense of needing to hurry in making a decision as to what life you would like next. In the spirit world we seem to have more courage, often taking on difficult life lessons that once incarnated seem very hard indeed. We also know that once this wheel of life is complete that we move closer to God and our real home. This is the incentive that keeps us evolving, always toward God's LOVE.

Rumi stated "We begin as a mineral. We emerge into plant life and into animal state, and then into being human, and always we have forgotten our former states, except in early spring when we slightly recall being green again." Meher Baba wrote an entire book on the reincarnation journey of our souls that mirrors Rumi. This reincarnation journey will eventually startle us back to the truth of who we are.

When one considers reincarnation, it is almost always in a linear fashion: going from lives in the past to lives in the future. Yet since there is no time in Reality all lives are occurring at the same time. Not only is this difficult for most to comprehend, it is also possible that all lifetimes have already occurred and our lives are but repeats: Thus the ideas of destiny or fate. When the thought of separation occurred by the One Son of God, it did not exist for even a nano-second and not even a note was missed in the song of God. It is as if all possible existences as separate identities rolled out like a carpet and then rolled right back up again. We are just reliving dreamed up lives that have already occurred and disappeared. Such is the explanation for the common experiences we have which we call déjà vu (feelings of familiarity) and Deja vecu (feelings of "already lived through" something).

What is the purpose of living in this dream when our real existence is with God because we never left? What is the purpose of reincarnation if it is all just a dream? In one sense it is like a virtual reality game we agree to play in this "Earth Plane" game to see if we can Awaken to the LOVE that we really are within a world that seems dominated by greed, sadness, pain, poverty, chaos, wars, etc., which is the result of the ego's system of separation: "kill or be killed." Can we be like the Prodigal Son, returning to the LOVE of God with a deeper spirituality?

The question we need to put to ourselves is: Can we be in this world but not of it? Can we express our innate beingness of LOVE in such an environment or do we get sucked into self-preservation at others' expense? Is our response to the trials of the physical plane one of self protection or is it expressions of our spiritual Self: peace, love, kindness, caring, giving, etc.?

Free will has to do with our choice of how we respond and live in the earthly dream. Not so much as to what we are doing, but how we are BEING. It is up to us to maintain an attitude of LOVE and acceptance. It is up to us to really want to return to the Love of God and rejoin Him in Heaven. Are we willing to give up our personal identity and exist in Spirit with God?

— CHAPTER TWENTY-FIVE —
THE WAY FORWARD

In an attempt to answer the big questions of our life here on Earth ("Who are we?" and "Why are we here?") we have explored every possible avenue. A partial list would include:

    Religion & Philosophy
    Chakra balance & Colonics
    Crystals & NLP
    Gurus & Workshops
    Psychics, Acupuncturists & Astrology
    Tribal Chants & Flower Remedies
    Subliminal Tapes & Life Coaches
    Enneagrams & the Elements of Man
    Meditation & Gestalt Therapy
    Go to India & Astral Projection
    Near Death Experiences & Hypnosis
    Etc.
    AND on and on

We have tried them all and yet most of us have not found the answer, not found our path to God realization. Even if we get close, have a brief flash of our connectedness to God, the ego comes rushing in with pride and our thoughts of separation continue.

We are continually looking for the right path that will bring us closer to God and to who we really are: the One Son of God. These heroic efforts do not work because the path is not "out there" someplace, but within us. In the book "King Without a Kingdom," the author spent most of his life looking outside for happiness and meaning only to realize much later in life that indeed the "Kingdom is Within." Yeshua was not the first to mention this inner path as the Gnostics had been following this precept years before Yeshua'a arrival. But Yeshua did preach it convincingly and so profoundly that it was included in the man-made Bible.

Violence in the world is but a reflection of violence in our minds. Changing our hearts will change our culture. Then generosity, compassion, and wisdom are the natural outcomes. Yeshua, Lao Tzu, Buddha, Ramana Maharshi, and most masters did not try to change the world, only our minds and hearts which in turn WILL change the world.

Who we are is the "Awareness of Love" as the sole descriptor. There need not be dependence on any teacher, although they can be helpful in providing direction. God is the inner dweller in all of us whether we are good or bad, a saint or a sinner. The only true LOVE is God's LOVE. God exists as our Self and is in every finite self. True Knowledge is not out there someplace, but within, and it is always present. It is only blocked by our identification with our ego thoughts and experiences that we mistakenly think are us.

What is available to all of us is our own freedom to choose what we have forgotten. It is not new or something that is needed to be acquired because it is already within us, just forgotten. Our Minds are free and whole and not limited. It is ours and available. We just need to rediscover it and reside there.

It is up to us to focus on who we really are as the Self with a capital "S" and away from the little self of the ego, which is our fear based personal identity. As the Persian poet, Rumi, stated some

800 years ago, "Everyone is headed back to God. If you want to quicken the journey, there are many paths." Let us all take the inner path and journey back to God. And as Kenneth Wapnick once told me "If this all seems confusing or difficult, just be kind…to everyone and everything. That is enough."

"WHO AM I?" The perennial question the inquirer keeps asking. I am a father, a husband, a developer, an American, a male, a golfer, a college graduate; we know ourselves only in relationship to something outside ourselves. But who are we prior to all these qualifications? If we want to know our true nature we should know who we are not; all of these outward identifications. Who we really are cannot be put into words because our real state of Being is nondual, absolute and constant presence whatever the circumstances. It can only be experienced. And the path to this constant knowing is always within.

WHO AM I?
- I am John
- And I have quite a story
- I have loved and lost
- Then…loved again
- Then…lost again
- Youth that would never end
- Has deserted me
- Children I nurtured and loved deeply
- Have flown away
- Structures I created
- Are applauded by a society that I no longer value
- My personal self and story are like smoke
- Dispersed by the wind
- Nothing remains

BUT wait. Who am I really?
- Am I more than my story of a separate self?
- There is a loud silence I hear deep within

- Beyond words or explanations
- A sense of Oneness with All
- Existing beyond John
- Where I am everyone and everything
- Way beyond my story
- Infinite, Immortal, Universal, Eternal
- Immersed in LOVE, ever extending
- One with All
- The Self I truly am

ABOUT THE AUTHOR

John Hulbert grew up in sunny Southern California, graduating from Newport Harbor High School and then from Occidental College with a BA degree in economics. He became interested in the metaphysical and spiritual after reading Paramahansa Yogananda's "Autobiography of a Yogi" and books by Edgar Cayce in the early 1970s. He became a student of Chung Fu (meaning Inner Truth from the I Ching), the spirit guide of medium Marshall Lever. For a period of five years he received information on the subconscious, Elements of Man, the 33 Energies, Jesus' historic life, childhood, and many other esoteric topics. He continued his study with teachers, books, workshops, meditation, retreats and the like throughout his life.

Through his work as a real estate developer he had the opportunity to live and study in different countries including the Fiji Islands, New Zealand, Paris, France, St. Martin in the Caribbean, as well as several states in the US. He presently lives in the foothills of the Sierra Mountains in Northern California.

John's years of studying spirituality, philosophy, psychology, and the new age movement was chronicled in his book *"King Without a Kingdom"* where he addressed the perennial questions of "Who am I?" and "Why am I here?"

Now he takes on the most important story of the last 2,000 years; the historical life and message of Yeshua.

John would be pleased to connect with you, the reader, to answer questions or receive comments. He can be contacted at his email: jahulbert33@gmail.com.

As an independent author, I thrive off your reviews. Would you take 5 minutes to leave a review for this book on Amazon, Goodreads, or wherever else you love to review books? Your thoughtful words will help future readers, and it is the greatest thanks you can give me, as the author, too.

Goodreads:
https://www.goodreads.com/book/show/44672089-king-without-a-kingdom?from_search=true

www.ingramcontent.com/pod-product-compliance
Lightning Source LLC
LaVergne TN
LVHW020930090426
835512LV00020B/3291